Students with Disabilities Can Meet Accountability Standards

A Road Map for School Leaders

John O'Connor

Published in partnership with the
American Association of School Administrators

ROWMAN & LITTLEFIELD EDUCATION
A division of
ROWMAN & LITTLEFIELD PUBLISHERS, INC.
Lanham • New York • Toronto • Plymouth, UK

Published in partnership with the American Association of School Administrators

Published by Rowman & Littlefield Education
A division of Rowman & Littlefield Publishers, Inc.
A wholly owned subsidary of The Rowman & Littlefield Publishing Group, Inc.
4501 Forbes Boulevard, Suite 200, Lanham, Maryland 20706
www.rowmaneducation.com

Estover Road, Plymouth PL6 7PY, United Kingdom

British Library Cataloguing in Publication Information Available

Library of Congress Cataloging-in-Publication Data

O'Connor, John, 1965–
  Students with disabilities can meet accountability standards : a roadmap for school leaders / John O'Connor.
    p. cm.
  Includes bibliographical references.
  ISBN 978-1-60709-470-8 (cloth : alk. paper) — ISBN 978-1-60709-471-5 (pbk. : alk. paper) — ISBN 978-1-60709-472-2 (electronic)
  1. Students with disabilities—Education. 2. Special education teachers—Training of. 3. Inclusive education. 4. Mainstreaming in education 5. Educational accountability. 6. Educational leadership. 7. Education—Standards. I. Title.

  LC4065.O27 2010
  371.9—dc22   2009025272

♾ ᵀᴹ The paper used in this publication meets the minimum requirements of American National Standard for Information Sciences—Permanence of Paper for Printed Library Materials, ANSI/NISO Z39.48-1992.

Printed in the United States of America

This book is dedicated to Shawn, J. T., and Luke and to all of the teachers, school leaders, and parents who constantly show us that students with disabilities can achieve great things.

Contents

List of Figures   vii

List of Tables   ix

Acknowledgments   xi

1 Students with Disabilities   1

2 GREAT Instruction: Guided by the Curriculum   15

3 Rigorous with Research-Based Strategies   21

4 Engaging and Exciting   45

5 Assessed Continuously to Guide Instruction   47

6 Tailored through Flexible Groups   51

7 Including More Students with Disabilities in General
   Education Classes   57

8 Behavioral Challenges   69

9 Changing Adult Practices   77

10 Aligning and Preparing the Leadership Team:
   Needs Assessment   85

11 Aligning and Preparing the Leadership Team:
   Common Expectations   93

12 Align All Programs and Initiatives toward
   GREAT Instruction   109

13 Equipping Teachers to Provide GREAT Instruction   113

14 Quit Doing Stuff That Doesn't Help   125

15 Unrelenting Persistence   141

References   145

About the Author   147

Figures

2.1. Gauge of Instruction   17

3.1. Array of Scores with Instruction Focused on Minimum
Passing Score   24

3.2. Array of Scores with Rigorous Instruction   24

Tables

7.1. Lake Shore School System—Did the Disability
Subgroup Make AYP?   60

10.1. GREAT Instruction Rating Scale   89–90

11.1. Observation/Coaching Tool   104–106

14.1. Percentage of Students Who Met/Exceeded Expectations
in Mathematics   129

14.2. Percentage of Students Who Met/Exceeded Expectations
in English/Language Arts   129

14.3. Percentage of Students Absent More Than Fifteen Days
during the School Year   129

Acknowledgments

I extend my appreciation to numerous colleagues and friends who have been generous with their knowledge through the years as we have worked together to improve the achievement of students with disabilities. I have learned countless lessons from the special education personnel at the Georgia Department of Education. They are diligent in their efforts to provide a balanced combination of support and accountability to local school systems across Georgia. I must also thank the personnel of the Georgia Learning Resources System. They set the bar in implementing effective professional development systems that improve adult practices, thereby ultimately impacting student achievement. I also express my thanks to the special education leaders in the DeKalb County School System. They work tirelessly to not only ensure that the daily operations of a large school system's special education program run smoothly, but they also take the necessary steps to make the systemic changes needed to radically improve student achievement.

I would specifically like to thank individuals who have given of their time and expertise to review this book and make valuable suggestions for improvement. I am indebted to Marie Corrigan, Tom Koerner, John O'Dell, Gloria Talley, Amy Vogt, and Lynne Williams. Your insight has improved this book immensely.

Chapter One

Students with Disabilities

In 2002, the educational landscape for students with disabilities was radically changed. The No Child Left Behind legislation created an accountability system for all schools that was based on student performance, including the performance of students with disabilities. The idea of grading schools based on student achievement was not shocking in and of itself. Several states had already implemented outcome-based accountability standards that judged schools based on the performance of their students. The newsworthy part of the legislation centered on how schools had to show progress and, more importantly, for whom.

In previous accountability measures, a school could show progress based on the school's averages (e.g., "My school is showing improvement because across my entire student body, 8 percent more students passed the end-of-the-year test"). The problem with this type of accountability was that some subgroups of students got lost in the average.

Once you dug into the data, it was obvious that some groups of students were performing quite well while other subgroups were being "left behind." Some ethnic groups were underperforming while other ethnic groups were showing progress. Students from economically disadvantaged homes were struggling while students from higher economic strata were showing gains.

In response to this, the No Child Left Behind legislation addressed each subgroup of students. No longer could a school only report gains across the school—the average; they had to report the progress of each subgroup of students. Those subgroups included the various ethnic groups (African American, American Indian, Asian, Hispanic, Pacific Islanders, White, etc.), students from economically disadvantaged circumstances, those with disabilities, and those who have limited English proficiency.

Not only did every school have to report the progress of each subgroup, but the school would be evaluated on the performance of each subgroup. In fact, if each subgroup did not meet specific benchmarks, then the school could eventually be labeled as a "needs improvement" school. Therefore, a school might show progress for every subgroup of students, but if the disability subgroup did not meet performance targets for multiple years, then the school could be labeled as a "needs improvement" school.

This type of accountability, by subgroup, was a radical departure for students with disabilities and those teachers and leaders who provided them with education programs. For the three decades prior to the No Child Left Behind legislation, students with disabilities were essentially removed from a school's accountability system. Individual students may have participated in the annual assessments, but their test answer sheets were marked with a special code so that their scores were not included in the school's testing results. In other cases, some students' Individualized Education Program (IEP) teams determined that they did not have to participate in the annual test at all.

Prior to the No Child Left Behind legislation, there was an accountability system in place for students with disabilities, but it was entirely unique for that population of students. The Individuals with Disabilities Education Improvement Act of 2004 (and the former versions of the law dating back to 1975) had clearly outlined specific actions that must be implemented for students with disabilities. Unfortunately, those hundreds and hundreds of stipulations focused entirely on processes, not student outcomes.

The Individuals with Disabilities Education Improvement Act (IDEA) legislation dictated the activities that must be implemented to: (1) correctly identify that a student has a disability, (2) the steps necessary to develop a plan for that student and the adults that must participate in the development of that plan, and (3) how often the student's disability should be reconsidered, and so forth. There is a valid need for most of these requirements, but they are exclusively focused on process activities that have to be implemented. The IDEA legislation is silent (or at least muffled) on any requirements to improve the performance of students with disabilities.

Therefore, there were really two isolated and independent accountability systems in our nation's schools. For students without disabilities, many states had moved toward accountability systems based on a school's ability to improve student performance. For students with disabilities, the IDEA legislation focused almost exclusively on process (paperwork) activities. There was a negative impact of those separate accountability systems. Students with disabilities were often left out when instructional innovations were implemented. School leaders did not intentionally disregard the needs of students with disabilities when adopting the latest textbook series or when providing professional development for teachers, but there was undoubtedly a disconnection.

Since the passage of the No Child Left Behind legislation, U.S. public schools have been operating under a unified accountability system in which every subgroup of students, including students with disabilities, is fully integrated into the accountability system. The truth is that the specifics of the requirements may change as accountability laws are reauthorized, but one thing is clear. Students with disabilities will be a critical component of any educational accountability system regardless of the name of the law or the year it will be authorized.

So after several years of outcome-based accountability, how are students performing? What does the data tell us about students with disabilities? Let's assume that two students, Juan and Michelle, have disabilities and receive special education services in a public school in the United States. What are the odds for these students? According to the United States Department of Education (2005),

- They have about a 50 percent chance of graduating high school with a general education diploma. In fact, in 2002–2003, 51.9 percent of students with disabilities in public schools across the country earned a "regular" high school diploma (not including special education diplomas or certificates of attendance).
- They have about a 30 percent chance of dropping out of high school. In fact, 33.6 percent of students with disabilities across the country dropped out of school.

What if these students are educated in different states? What are the "odds" for these students?

- In California, they have a high probability that they will not be successful in math or English/language arts. Sixty-two percent of students with disabilities who were in the third through eighth grades did not meet expectations in mathematics on the California Standards Test. Seventy-seven percent of students with disabilities did not meet expectations in English/language arts on the same assessment (California Department of Education 2007).
- If they live in Illinois, the odds are very low that they will be successful in high school mathematics. Approximately 15 percent of students with disabilities in the eleventh grade met or exceeded expectations on the math subtest of the Prairie State Achievement Examination (Illinois State Board of Education 2008).

• In Georgia, they have a suppressed chance of earning a high school diploma. Only 37.7 percent of students with disabilities earn a general education diploma (Georgia Department of Education 2008a).

Regardless of the state that is analyzed, the data are similar. Students with
disabilities are underperforming when compared to other subgroups. The
good news, however, is that students with disabilities, by and large, have
made significant progress. Even though these data may leave something to be
desired, across most states, the data reflect progress. In fact, in some states,
students with disabilities are the subgroup that is gaining the most ground.

Even though there is progress to be made, the teachers, school leaders, and
parents who are working every day to support and educate students with disabilities should be commended for their work.

These data require deeper analyses. There are thirteen categories of disabilities according to the Individuals with Disabilities Education Improvement Act of 2004. There are visual impairments, orthopedic impairments,
other health impairments, emotional/behavioral disorders, and so on. When
disaggregating this type of data, some patterns become apparent. Students
with emotional/behavioral disabilities, for example, have a higher dropout
rate and a lower rate of earning a general education diploma than do students
with visual impairments. Students with speech impairments (as their only
disability category or primary disability) show high achievement when compared to students with other disabilities.

Even though there has been significant progress, the data are clear. There is
a great opportunity for improvement. Consider for example that only half of
students with disabilities across the country earn a general education diploma.
After twelve or so years in public school, these students have not earned the
gateway document that will enable them to have a variety of options after
their high school years.

Without a regular high school diploma, students with disabilities are not
able to gain entry into most four-year colleges. They are not able to participate in the military, and in most cases they are not granted entry into technical
schools. Their options become very limited. They are only equipped to gain
entry-level employment. Unfortunately, their options for moving "up in the
company" will be very limited because they do not have a regular diploma
and will be competing for promotions against other individuals who have
high school diplomas or postsecondary training.

Some individuals might say that the concern over the apparent underperformance of students with disabilities is counterintuitive. Students with
disabilities are underperforming because they have disabilities after all. That
does seem to make a certain amount of sense. Students only receive special

education services if they have demonstrated an area of disability (e.g., academic, intellectual, sensory) to such a level that they require special education services. By definition, students with disabilities struggle in some way in school.

There are two problems with this logic. First, approximately 80 percent of students with disabilities have average intelligence (Gloeckler 2006). If students have average intelligence, then they have average potential. They have the intellectual potential to master grade-level material. They can understand the work. They may have physical, sensory, or learning differences that must be accommodated, but their fundamental capacity is there.

The second flaw with the logic is that annual statewide assessments that are the foundation of most state's accountability systems are not extremely rigorous. Nor is the number of correct answers required to "pass" the test very high. These tests are designed to show minimal competency standards. What are the minimal standards that a third grader should show at the end of the year? What is the lowest, passable standard?

In many states, these tests are gateway tests, at least for some grades. Students cannot be promoted to the next grade or earn a regular high school diploma unless they pass the test. In that scenario, the respective state department of education, or similar governing body, had to design tests that were meant to show minimal competency. You can't keep a child from earning his high school diploma by giving him an extremely difficult test.

The "passing score" on the tests is usually very low. In some states, students only have to answer about half of the questions correctly in order to receive a passing score. If you only have to pass half of the questions on a multiple-choice test that typically has four choices per question, then the demand is certainly not too high for most students with disabilities.

Considering that an overwhelming majority of students with disabilities have average intelligence, and therefore the intellectual potential to meet academic standards, and that the expectations on many statewide assessments are low, isn't it possible that a higher percentage of students with disabilities can meet the requirements of schools' accountability systems?

This premise leaves public schools in a challenging position. What should schools do to increase the academic achievement of students with disabilities so that they have a wide variety of meaningful options after high school? What can school personnel do to meet the accountability standards for students with disabilities so that their school is considered a high-performing school rather than a school that is labeled "needs improvement"?

The purpose of this book is to enable school personnel to effectively educate students with disabilities so that they meet academic standards. Perhaps surprisingly, this book is not targeted for special education teachers. In fact, that would be an ineffective way to improve the performance of students with disabilities across a school. In fact, according to the U.S. Department of Education, approximately half of all students with disabilities spend at least 80 percent of their school day in "general education" classes.

In a school in which there are six periods in a school day, those students would spend at least five of those segments in general education classes with their nondisabled peers. For the other period, the student may be educated in a special education classroom.

Because of this type of inclusion for students with disabilities, there are students with disabilities in practically every classroom in public schools. In fact, it is somewhat difficult to find a general education class in which at least one of the students does not receive special education services. If we are going to improve the performance of students with disabilities, then we have to influence all adults throughout the school—all teachers from every classroom and all school leaders.

Therefore, this book is designed for those individuals in our public schools who have an impact on the performance of students with disabilities—general education teachers, special education teachers, principals, assistant principals, counselors, psychologists, department chairs, and so on. In fact, this book is specifically designed for a team of individuals, an expanded school leadership team, who will have great influence on the entire school so that we can improve the achievement of students with disabilities across the school.

This book has two main purposes. The first half of the book clearly describes the instructional practices that will have the greatest impact on the achievement of students with disabilities. This includes specific instructional components that should occur in every class across the school whether the classrooms are general education classes or special education classes. (This book is focused on the 80 percent of students with disabilities who have average intelligence. Even though the needs of other students with disabilities are critical, they are not the focus of this book.)

The second half of the book includes a description of how to change the practices of the adults in the school so that you see those preferred instructional practices. Most instructional initiatives fail because they are not implemented well. The new textbooks or instructional strategies are presented in professional development activities, but they do not make their way to full implementation in classrooms.

This book is designed not only to describe the instructional activities that must be seen routinely in classrooms across the school, but also to provide a step-by-step process to ensure that those instructional activities become embedded in every classroom across the school. This book includes specific steps in how to provide the necessary consensus building, professional development, coaching, and support so that each member of your faculty, in their respective roles, is effective at either leading the instruction across the school or providing classroom instruction that will meet the needs of students with disabilities.

EXPANDING THE MEMBERS OF THE LEADERSHIP TEAM

Throughout this book, there are Questions for Reflection at the conclusion of each chapter. The questions are designed to help the reader analyze the activities of his or her school and to plot a path for improvement. It is ideal to read this book and complete the postchapter questions with an expanded leadership team from your school.

I had an interesting experience lately. While working with a school district, I met with the equivalent of the special education department chairpersons from the school district's high schools. I asked if they were part of their school's leadership team. They emphatically said no. I was asking about the group of leaders in their school who work together to analyze students' ongoing performance and provide concrete instructional leadership to their school. A few days later, I had the opportunity to meet with several of the high school principals. I asked them if the special education department chairpersons were on their school's leadership team. They emphatically said yes.

The conflict with the two perceptions centers on the role of the leadership team. The special education department chairs had been in many meetings with their principal's lead administrators, but those meetings had not focused on continually reviewing ongoing student performance data to determine how students are performing. Their group did not take the results of data and then provide professional development, coaching, or consultation to their teachers so that instructional and classroom practices are improved. The special education department chairs assumed that there was another leadership group in the building who were conducting the rigorous work of improving student achievement.

Yet the principals held the perception that they had a leadership team and that team included the special education department chairs. Their leadership team, unfortunately, did not primarily focus on improving student learning as described above. Even though student achievement may be discussed, their primary focus was to discuss the management of the school (e.g., transportation, school functions, extracurricular activities, and various school-related procedures). These principals may have been under the impression that those discussions were about instructional leadership. As critical as those discussions are, they are not the discussions that must take place to radically improve student achievement for any group, much less the students with disabilities, across the school.

In order to improve the achievement of students with disabilities, the activities and existing membership of your expanded leadership team must be addressed. You must ensure that they are devoting a significant amount of time to: (1) analyzing current instructional and classroom practices and the performance of students, (2) developing interventions that will respond to that information, and (3) implementing change activities in the school. Sometimes those changes will be structural in nature, such as changing the school's master schedule. At other times, they will be instructional in nature. The team may need to provide professional development, ongoing coaching, and continual monitoring to assist teachers as they change their practices (a process that will be discussed at length later in this book).

Your leadership team that addresses the instructional needs of students with disabilities in your school should not be a unique group of leaders set aside for this purpose. In fact, the team that addresses the needs of students with disabilities should be the same team that addresses the instructional needs of all of the students. If your school already has a team that routinely and systematically works to improve student achievement, then your existing group should complete the process described in this book to ensure that they are addressing the needs of all students, including students with disabilities.

You may need to expand the membership of your team to adequately address the needs of students with disabilities. If you are developing a leadership team for the first time, you must ensure that the membership is equipped to address the issues appropriately. Not only do the members have to have the knowledge of the issues at hand regarding students with disabilities, but they must also have the resources and influence. Therefore, whether you are expanding the membership of your existing leadership team or developing a team for the first time, a list of the required members and the rationale for their selection is provided below.

That team should include the principal, assistant principals, counselors, central office representatives, and teacher leaders (general education and special education) from every department or grade in the school. The selection of the individual members of the leadership team will be very important as you work through this book. Their roles in this process will be very specific depending on their position.

Principal

The principal has a unique role and must lead the team's effort. The principal sets the tone of urgency and expectations for the entire school. The principal should provide clear direction and expectations for the leadership team and the rest of the staff. *This role cannot be delegated.* Many school initiatives have failed because they have been completely driven by someone other than the principal, like the assistant principal.

Unfortunately, the assistant principal, no matter how talented, does not warrant the same attention as the principal. The message of urgency and priority must come from the principal. The principal must stand in front of the school faculty and stress the importance of the initiative and clearly articulate the expectations for the school. He or she can make it clear repeatedly that in his or her school, there will be an unwavering focus on improving and fine-tuning classroom instruction.

The details of the initiative can be delegated to other personnel, but the principal must set the foundation and expectations. The school staff will only participate in school improvement efforts, including the process described in this book, to the extent that the principal leads the effort and emphasizes its importance.

The principal will also set the bar for students with disabilities by clearly articulating that students with disabilities can achieve at high levels. He or she must ensure that all faculty members set high expectations for students with disabilities and enable those students to reach those expectations.

If the principal sets the tone that students with disabilities are unable to meet high expectations, then the school staff will not consistently tinker with instructional practices until those expectations are met. They will assume that underperformance is inevitable and therefore be unwilling to critically examine existing instructional practices and ongoing student performance to make mid-course adjustments.

On the other hand, if the principal sets the tone for high expectations, then the leaders and teachers will not be satisfied with low levels of achievement. They will continually brainstorm and collaborate until instructional practices are adjusted in the most efficient way to produce high achievement.

Assistant Principals

All of the assistant principals in your school (regardless of their title) should also participate in this process. In many larger schools, there are assistant principals for instruction, for attendance, for discipline, and so forth. Unfortunately, a barrier has been created with those titles. Many school personnel assume that improving classroom practices is the sole responsibility of the administrator whose title includes the term "instruction." In other schools, one particular assistant principal is responsible for improving the performance of students with disabilities with a title such as Assistant Principal for Special Populations.

Many teachers (and many assistant principals themselves) believe that none of the other assistant principals bear any responsibility for improving classroom practices across the school or improving the achievement of students with disabilities. All assistant principals are responsible for improving classroom practices throughout the school. They are also all responsible for improving the achievement of students with disabilities.

All administrators need to be in the game. They must work together to provide consistent support and coaching to teachers as they try new instructional techniques and reflect on those strategies. All administrators, including all assistant principals, must be transformed from school administrators to instructional leaders.

Support Personnel

The expanded leadership team should also include support personnel such as counselors, school psychologists, and the like. Even though they may not be directly responsible for classroom instruction, they play a unique and important role in improving student achievement. This group may discuss students with disabilities who have significant emotional and behavioral challenges. In that case, counselors and psychologists will bring their specialized expertise to discussions about interventions.

Including support personnel in this group also sends an extremely important message. Nobody is exempt from improving the performance of students with disabilities. If any certified or licensed personnel suggest that their job does not impact student performance, then it is worthwhile to analyze the impact they are having at the school and their understanding of their role and responsibilities.

Teachers

Teachers are perhaps the most important members of the expanded leadership team. At the end of the day, they are the personnel who are providing the instruction in classrooms. General education and special education teachers have unique areas of expertise that are needed during the conversations that will occur after each chapter. Typically (although it is certainly not universal), general education teachers have more training in their respective content area. Special education teachers typically have more training and expertise in matching specific instructional strategies to students' areas of need. Both areas of expertise are critical to improving the achievement of students with disabilities.

There must be some careful consideration when choosing which teachers to include in the expanded leadership team. In addition to department chairs, representatives from each area (e.g., special education and English Language Learners), and other official teacher leaders, the team should include teachers who have great influence. Some super-teachers have a positive impact on any initiative in the school. They continually volunteer for extra activities and find a way to "get the job done" regardless of the challenges that arise. They should definitely be included on the leadership team.

Other teachers who have influence, perhaps even negative influence, should also be included on the leadership team. There are some teachers in many schools who have taught at the school for many years, have long-standing institutional knowledge, and have strong influences on other teachers. They may even express resistance to most new ideas. Those teachers should be on the leadership team that works through this book. As long as their influence is not negative to the point of being poisonous, it is critical to gain their acceptance on the front end of this initiative rather than trying to convince them of its value at a later date.

Internal and External Helpers

The leadership team that works together to complete this book should also include internal and external helpers. Instructional coaches, whether they are full-time school employees or based at the central office, should participate in this process. Regardless of the title in your school, the instructional coaches often receive direction from professionals outside of your school and bring effective ideas back to your school. Unfortunately, it is easy for their activities, no matter how sound, to lack alignment with your initiatives.

If they participate in your school's process for building effective instructional practices, then they can bring their new ideas to the leadership group and work in alignment with your efforts. Their efforts will be implemented through the lens and overall plan of your efforts, rather than competing with your initiatives.

Your leadership team should include at least one professional from the central office. It may be appropriate to include a central office special education administrator. Like the instructional coaches, their ownership of the ultimate plan to improve instruction will strengthen your efforts. In many school districts, central office personnel are aware of resources that are available that can contribute to your team's efforts to improve instruction. They may be aware of funding sources, individuals with expertise, and initiatives that would fold effectively into your overall efforts. With their knowledge base and connections, central office personnel can contribute to the growth of your leadership team and the ultimate implementation of any school improvement initiative.

As your team works through this book, they will follow the steps that are outlined in the following visual organizer. It answers a main, overarching question and two subquestions. The unifying question is, "How do we radically improve the achievement of students with disabilities?" The subquestions are:

- What will it look like?
- How do we make it happen?

Textbox 1.1.   Increasing the Achievement of Students with Disabilities

What should it look like?

Provide GREAT instruction in every classroom. GREAT instruction is:
- Guided by the curriculum.
- Rigorous with research-based strategies (e.g., National Reading Panel, National Math Advisory Panel, Explicit Instruction, Vocabulary Instruction, Visual Organizers, etc.).
- Engaging and Exciting.
- Assessed continuously to guide instruction.
- Tailored through flexible groups.

- Increase the percentage of students with disabilities who are taught in general education classes.
- When co-teaching is used, implement preferred teaching models.
- Provide filling-the-gaps instruction with effectiveness.

Address behavioral challenges.
- Provide rituals and routines consistently.
- Establish and teach expectations.
- Provide reinforcement, encouragement, and rewards abundantly.
- Use redirection and consequences efficiently.
- Conduct formal and informal Functional Behavioral Assessments and develop Behavior Intervention Plans.

How do we make it happen?

Conduct a needs analysis.
- Analyze quantitative student data.
- Analyze qualitative data of classroom practices.

As the expanded leadership team, develop common expectations for:
- Each element of GREAT instruction.
- Co-teaching instruction.
- Filling-the-gaps instruction.
- Practices to improve student behavior.

Equip teachers to provide GREAT instruction.
- Implement formative assessments across the school.
- Utilize teacher teams to analyze formative assessment results.
- Expand the teachers' conversation—flexible grouping.
- Provide explicit training on instructional strategies.
- Provide monitoring and coaching of classroom practices.
- Support high-need teachers.
- Promote teacher-to-teacher peer observations.

Quit doing stuff that doesn't help.
- Discontinue ineffective professional development practices.
- Make annual planning meaningful.
- Focus on instruction, not process.
- Focus on changing practices, not culture.

It may seem that unifying such an expansive team to improve the performance of students with disabilities is somewhat excessive, especially considering that students with disabilities may only represent 10 percent or so of the student population in your school. The truth is that you should not develop a new leadership team to complete this book. Almost all schools have a working leadership team that completes an annual school improvement plan and meets regularly to discuss instruction. You should use that group to implement the practices in this book. You are not duplicating efforts.

In addition, the work of this team will have an impact on a much wider group of students than students with disabilities. Your efforts will be worthwhile. Your work will help all students in the school who struggle for various reasons. In fact, virtually all school personnel know that there are many students who struggle academically, socially, behaviorally, or in other ways and who do not have a disability label.

There is only a fine line between those students who are determined to have a disability in public schools and those students who struggle but do not meet the criteria for an educational disability. Experienced teachers realize that they may have two students who are almost identical in their classroom struggles but have one very significant difference. Because of the complex ways in which students "qualify" for special education, one of those students might have an educational disability while the other student does not.

While the leadership team completes this book, they will become competent in implementing school activities that will not only help students with disabilities, but will also help all of the other students in their school who struggle.

Questions for Reflection

In your school, who are the members of the leadership team that will answer the questions at the end of each chapter? Include all administrators, support personnel, department chairs, other teacher leaders, and teachers who represent various programs in the school. Include all teachers who have significant influence on their colleagues. In addition, include internal and external instructional coaches who work in your school and central office personnel whose connections and knowledge can contribute to your efforts.

Chapter Two

GREAT Instruction:
Guided by the Curriculum

Our challenge is perfectly clear. Seeing that students with disabilities are fully integrated into the accountability system (not to mention that most students with disabilities have at least average potential), how do we radically increase achievement levels? If we could only focus on one thing, what one thing would impact the achievement of all students with disabilities? What one factor contributes to the success of students with disabilities above all other factors?

The truth is that there is one element in our schools that has the most robust history of changing student performance and it can be made available in every classroom. The one and only way to radically increase the achievement of students with disabilities is to provide great instruction. In fact, for decades, research has been very clear. The instruction provided in our nation's classrooms has a greater impact on student performance than anything else.

We know that students with disabilities and other students who struggle need great instruction, but truth be told, some children can probably at least meet standards with mediocre instruction. A small percentage of children actually learn to read spontaneously. When they are about three years old, they look at a book and realize that they have broken the code. All of those lines that used to look like squiggles now mean something. Those lines are letters. Those letters spell out words and those words tell a story.

Lynn Holland (personal communication, November 9, 2005) remembers that magical moment when she was three years old and it happened to her. She opened a book and all of a sudden, she could read. She remembers running down the hallway and telling her mother that she could read the book. She even remembers that it was a Winnie the Pooh book. How amazing!

To be honest, children who come to school with these skills can probably do well with passable instruction, especially in their primary school years.

They may not meet their potential without great instruction, but they will demonstrate sufficient achievement with mediocre instruction. Other children, especially those students who have disabilities, need great instruction. In fact, nothing else will make a significant impact on the academic achievement of all students with disabilities and other students who struggle.

What are the components of "great" instruction? If each of the teachers in your school was asked what constitutes great instruction, how many answers would you get? In many schools, you would get as many answers as you have teachers. Why do public schools allow every teacher to determine the components of great instruction? That seems like an inefficient way to move in the same direction. Are the teachers in your school working extremely hard but lacking efficiency because they are implementing instructional strategies that are less than effective?

A combination of research- and school-based experiences tells us that there are specific components that make up great instruction. GREAT instruction is:

- **G**uided by the curriculum
- **R**igorous with **r**esearch-based strategies
- **E**ngaging and **e**xciting
- **A**ssessed continuously to guide instruction, and
- **T**ailored through flexible groups.

You may ask, "What is so special about GREAT instruction? Don't students with disabilities need something else? How is the need for GREAT instruction different for students with disabilities than it is for students without disabilities?"

For years, we thought that students with disabilities needed something completely different than their peers without disabilities. A child who was determined to have an educational disability was often taken out of the curriculum that was used by all other students. We automatically provided different textbooks and different classrooms for many students with disabilities.

Fortunately, we now know that an overwhelming number of students with disabilities need the same thing that other students need, but the difference is that students with disabilities need it more intensely. There is much less room for error. Students with disabilities who have significant emotional and behavioral needs, for example, need targeted and intensive behavioral systems in which they receive reinforcement more frequently and more intensely than other students. All students need explicit instruction in behavioral expectations and reinforcement that helps promote responsible behaviors. Students

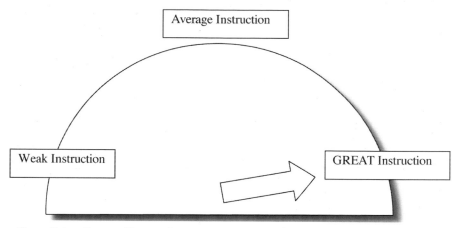

Figure 2.1.   Gauge of Instruction

with disabilities need those same things. They just need those things with more expertise and intensity.

The same thing applies to instruction for students with disabilities. The instruction must be targeted and extremely efficient. On the proverbial gauge of GREAT instruction, students with disabilities and other students who struggle need the gauge to rest solely on the "far right." For some high-achieving students and even average students, the instruction gauge can be somewhat to the left and they may still achieve; not so for students with disabilities.

For each element of GREAT instruction, students with disabilities must receive top-notch instruction that is delivered with extreme focus and expertise. So what are the elements of GREAT instruction?

GUIDED BY THE CURRICULUM

GREAT instruction must be guided by the curriculum. In most states, there is a curriculum that has been defined by the state department of education. That curriculum has specific performance standards that clearly outline the expectations for children in different subjects and in different grades. Instruction should be aligned to the performance standards in that curriculum. School districts usually have some flexibility in the choice of materials and textbooks that are adopted to address that curriculum.

Unfortunately, in many classrooms, teachers assume that their curriculum is defined by the textbook series. They complete chapter after chapter in the text and therefore believe they are appropriately addressing the curriculum.

In fact, those materials are merely tools that can be used to assist students in mastering the components or standards of the curriculum.

Teachers need to have a deep knowledge of the competencies that students are expected to master by the end of the course or school year. They need to have a clear understanding of what the finish line looks like. They need to know how children will demonstrate those skills and competencies. They need to know when that demonstration is sufficiently complex to meet the expected standard.

Just as important, they need to have a clear understanding of when that demonstration of skillfulness does not meet the expectancy of the standard. What is the very fine line between being competent in each standard and being just below the bar? On the other end of the performance continuum, how can a student demonstrate performance that exceeds the curricular standards? How can students rise above the expectations and demonstrate even deeper understanding and skillfulness? What is the end point for those who can meet that greater challenge?

A thorough understanding of the curriculum prepares teachers for their day-to-day work with their students. If instruction is developed and delivered for the purpose of achieving the curricular standards, then teachers will be able to identify the students who are not on track to meet those standards a few weeks into instruction.

Through that deep knowledge and clear alignment with the curriculum, teachers will be able to alter instruction depending on the students' progress. They will be able to ramp up instruction when it is necessary, re-teach material at other times, and expect more complexity when students need more challenges. With a clear understanding and vision of the curricular standards, teachers can build effective instructional activities that lead to successfully reaching academic expectations.

It may be difficult to remember, but it was approximately ten years ago that each state's curriculum was somewhat irrelevant for students with disabilities. As mentioned previously, there was a time in which students with disabilities were not included in the accountability systems that were in place for all other students. Because of this, there was a big disconnection between each state's curriculum and the instruction that was provided to many students with disabilities. In fact, if special education teachers were asked, "What is that student learning in school?" most special education teachers would answer, "He is learning what is on his IEP."

In 1975, the Education for All Handicapped Children Act was passed as the first federal legislation that governed the provision of special education services for students with disabilities. One of the hallmarks of that legislation was the requirement that each student with a disability would have an Individualized Education Program (IEP) developed for that child that reflected the specific needs resulting from the disability.

Individualized Educational Program

The IEP, which has been included in each reauthorization of that original legislation, includes a description of the student's strengths and weaknesses, how the disability impacts educational performance, goals for the student, what special education services will be provided, and where those services would be provided (i.e., general education class versus a special education class). The IEP is developed by those adults who know the child the best, the student's educators and parents. In many ways, the IEP has been a very positive way to develop a unique plan for each child with a disability.

Unfortunately, the IEP has also had a negative impact. For nearly three decades, it was considered the authoritative document for what the student should be learning. School personnel taught the students toward the goals in the IEPs rather than the standards in the curriculum. At the end of the day, the handful of adults who wrote the IEP developed a curriculum for each individual student with a disability, a task that is beyond the skills of any handful of adults.

Each state's curricular standards are typically developed over many months (if not a few years) through a collaborative effort between subject experts, school administrators, teachers, parents, university personnel, and community members. It is then reviewed by countless committees and ultimately approved by a state board of education or similar body. Developing the curriculum in any one subject for merely one grade level is an expanded and arduous process.

For three decades (as driven by federal law), a disservice was done to many students with disabilities. A small group of adults were asked to develop a curriculum, which was an expectation well beyond their expertise (as it would be for any small group of adults). The IEP committee replaced the expansive expertise of the designers of the state curriculum. In essence, students with disabilities were essentially removed from the "general curriculum" and provided a weak replacement through the goals that were outlined on their respective IEPs.

Fortunately, we have made progress. The overwhelming majority of students with disabilities must participate in the state-mandated curriculum. They are also tested on that curriculum with the same statewide test as their nondisabled peers. Therefore, the IEPs no longer dictate what should be taught for students with disabilities. The curriculum is the focus. The IEPs now focus on those services and supports that must be put in place to enable students with disabilities to meet those curricular expectations.

Questions for Reflection

1. Across your school, is the instruction in every classroom driven by the curricular standards? Are both the general education teachers and the special education teachers effective in providing instruction that is driven by the standards?
2. Do all teachers (general education and special education) have a deep knowledge and expertise in the curricular standards?
3. Are IEPs adequately designed and implemented to enable students with disabilities to successfully reach the curricular standards?

Chapter Three

Rigorous with Research-Based Strategies

GREAT instruction should also be rigorous. Many people assume that students with disabilities need less rigorous instruction than their nondisabled peers. That, in fact, is quite wrong.

RIGOR—COVERING MORE GROUND

Students with disabilities need more rigorous instruction. Schools need to provide instruction that will allow them to catch up to their peers. They will have to learn at a faster rate than their classmates who are on grade level. The students not only need to master the same curricular standards as their peers, but they must also fill in those academic holes that they have developed over time, and in some cases meet other needs, such as learning Braille for a student who has a visual impairment.

They may need to be explicitly taught learning strategies to attack math word problems when other students may attain those metacognitive skills fairly naturally. They may need to be taught how to decode multisyllabic words when other students already have those skills. They may need to learn organizations skills when other students already know how to break down tasks to increase learning. Students with disabilities and other students who struggle need to learn more than other students in the same amount of time. Therefore, their instruction needs to be more rigorous, not less so.

The first way to ensure that students with disabilities have an opportunity to cover more ground is to ensure that time is maximized. In some classrooms and schools, there is a tremendous amount of downtime. Significant time is wasted as students enter a classroom, as materials are distributed, as the teacher waits for all students to enter the classroom to get settled. Time is also wasted near the end of the period as some teachers end the lesson about ten to fifteen minutes before the end of class so that students can begin their transition to their next class.

Since most students with disabilities are behind their nondisabled peers academically, there isn't a minute to waste. In every class, both general education classes and special education classes, activities should be waiting for students as they enter the classroom. They should walk in the room and get started—no milling around and no downtime.

In many classes, activities are provided for students when they enter the classroom, but they lack an appropriate level of rigor. There may be a low-level worksheet waiting for students. In that case, the teacher is setting the tone that students are expected to begin working at the start of the period. Unfortunately, the instructional activity isn't providing much benefit to the students.

In other classes, the students get settled for a while until the teacher can complete his or her class roll, adjust materials, and then address the class. Unfortunately, valuable time is wasted and it sets the tone that learning cannot happen in isolation of the teacher's instruction.

Every minute of every class period must be maximized. If a middle school student with a disability is reading two years below his chronological age, then every minute must be used in the most efficient way possible so that the student has an authentic opportunity to fill in all of the gaps in his learning and meet the grade-level curricular expectations.

Amanda Ripley from *Time* magazine articulates this sense of urgency with eloquence: "Great teachers are in total control. They have clear expectations and rules, and they are consistent with rewards and punishments. *Most of all, they are in a hurry.* They never feel that there is enough time in the day. They quiz kids on their multiplication tables while they walk to lunch. And they don't give up on their worst students, even when any normal person would" (Ripley 2008; italics added).

RIGOR—HIGH EXPECTATIONS

In addition to the need to cover more ground in the same time, students with disabilities need the rigor that every other student needs. All students should become sophisticated problem solvers—all students at all grade levels. We, as educational leaders and teachers, can only reach that goal with rigorous instruction and high expectations. First-grade instruction as well as instruction for seniors in high schools should include opportunities for students to attempt solutions to various challenges and to weigh those solutions against the challenge. Expectations should be developmentally appropriate for the students at various ages while promoting the use of higher-order thinking skills rather than surface-level information.

This focus on rigorous instruction may be somewhat different than what has been expected of students with disabilities in many schools. Unfortunately, it has not been uncommon to see a low hum of expectations for students with disabilities. The expectations and the corresponding low levels of rigor have unfortunately placed a false ceiling for many students with disabilities, resulting in lower performance which reinforced lower expectations. It is past time to break this cycle!

With a large majority of students with disabilities having average intelligence, it is our responsibility as educators to unlock students' potential and determine how we can provide instruction that allows them to meet high expectations.

RIGOR—RISING TIDES RAISE ALL SHIPS

Suppressed expectations, and therefore a lack of rigorous instruction, have also manifested themselves in another way. Many schools are aiming much too low for all students across the school by focusing almost exclusively on meeting the minimum required score on the statewide assessments. You will hear entire faculties talk about the magical "passing" score on the state test. Unfortunately, that passing score is what it takes for a student to show that he or she barely meets grade-level expectations. In many states, that bar is surprisingly low.

Focusing on the minimum proficiency score can actually decrease student achievement. Instead of solely striving to assist struggling students and students with disabilities to meet that minimum mark, schools should strive toward getting more students to significantly exceed that score. If more students exceed expectations, then all students, including students with disabilities, will surpass the minimum score.

In addition to "pushing" students from the tail end of the spectrum to just pass the test, school personnel should also "pull" the top students into even higher ranges so that all students shift to a higher level of performance. All students show growth and therefore all scores shift upward. Students who are doing well continue to show growth and students who are struggling meet or exceed the minimum requirements.

Take a look at the array of scores from a hypothetical school that focuses solely on assisting the students make the minimum passing score of 800 on

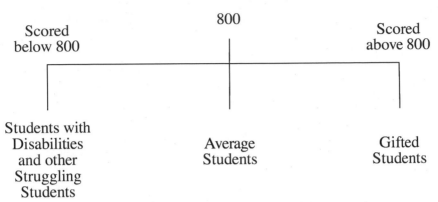

Figure 3.1.   Array of Scores with Instruction Focused on Minimum Passing Score

their statewide assessment. All teachers instruct all students in the hope that they will score at least 800 points on the annual assessment.

As a result of the teachers focusing on the minimum passing score, average students scored 800 points on the assessment and gifted students surpassed that score. Unfortunately, students with disabilities and other students who struggle scored below 800 points. Now look at the same hypothetical school if the teachers increase their rigor and "teach toward" the complexity of a score of 840 points.

When teachers increased the rigor in their instruction and aimed for a score of 840 for all students, then the average students reached 840, the gifted students exceeded that score, and many students with disabilities met and exceeded the state-defined minimum score of 800 points. (Some students with disabilities also exceeded standards.) Essentially, all scores were moved to the right. These teachers pulled from the top as well as pushed from the

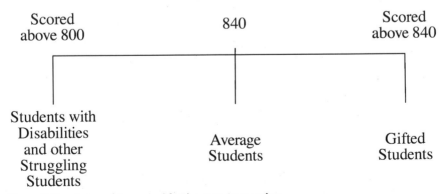

Figure 3.2.   Array of Scores with Rigorous Instruction

bottom. Previously, they had only pushed students in order to get them over the 800-point threshold.

At the end of the day, the array of scores in many schools will remain relatively stable. There may be a 50-point range that accounts for children ranging from the tenth percentile to the ninetieth percentile. This range will remain relatively constant. In order to assist students with disabilities and other struggling students to surpass the minimum passing score, then the entire range of scores must show progress. Therefore, instruction must be rigorous enough to allow all students to improve their performance and move the range "to the right."

How can rigorous instruction and high expectations be ensured in every classroom? Rigorous instruction must start with the teachers' knowledge of the content area. According to the United States Department of Education (2006), research indicates that there is a connection between teachers' knowledge of their content area and their students' levels of achievement.

Mathematics teachers, for example, must understand the complexities of their subject matter. They must be able to connect the various mathematical concepts at a deep level. It is not sufficient for mathematics teachers to merely understand how to compute figures. They must understand how various operations interact and relate. They must have a deep understanding of mathematical concepts and sophisticated problem-solving skills.

A science teacher must not be one chapter ahead of his or her students. The teacher must understand how science impacts all facets of life and should connect those everyday experiences with underlying scientific principles.

This requirement for expertise in the curriculum content has presented a problem for many special education teachers who hold a bachelor's or postgraduate degree in special education, not in the specific subject matter. They may have deep training in the pedagogy and instructional needs of students with unique disabilities, but they may lack extensive training in third-grade reading or high school biology, for example, and therefore be less prepared to provide expert instruction in the subject matter.

Therefore, as we move toward providing GREAT instruction for every student with a disability, we must provide opportunities for special education teachers (and some general education teachers) to gain expertise in their respective subject matter. We must equip them with a broad and deep knowledge of the subjects they are teaching. We need to allow all teachers to develop real expertise. Through the course of their careers, they should be engaged in activities that continually deepen their knowledge of their subject matter.

They should be challenged by other experts in their subject matter, some of whom will be teachers and some of whom may be scientists, researchers, or business professionals, who apply that content knowledge to everyday challenges in their work. Teachers not only need to provide rigorous instruction in their classroom, but they must also be learners in rigorous discussion, instruction, and problem solving. Teachers need to start every new school year with a broad base of experiences that they gathered over the summer that enriched their understanding of their subject matter. GREAT instruction hinges on teachers having a deep understanding of their subject matter so that they can provide rigorous and expert instruction for their students.

Unfortunately, there is a common misinterpretation regarding rigorous instruction. Some teachers and school leaders assume that providing rigorous instruction is merely the practice of expecting higher performance from students. They assume that having a harder class is equivalent to providing rigorous instruction. Some teachers, in fact, particularly in high schools, might brag that relatively few students make high grades (e.g., "The average grade in my science class was a 72").

Rigor does not reduce the obligation of the teacher to provide systematic and clear instruction. Merely offering harder work is not sufficient. Increased rigor must be accompanied with scaffolded instruction that will enable students to meet the heightened expectations.

The high school teacher who brags about the low performance rate of the students should reflect on why more students did not succeed. Explicit and systematic instruction and support should be built so that students are able to meet rigorous expectations.

What should rigorous instruction look like in our nation's classrooms, whether they are general education or special education classrooms? Teachers often speak of asking students to use higher-order thinking skills, but in actuality there are many teachers who do not routinely provide activities that will ensure that students become sophisticated problem solvers. This lack of rigor is often seen in middle and high school math classes.

At the beginning of the class, it is very common to see the math teacher ask the students to pull out their homework for a review. The teacher ensures that students completed their homework and then he or she demonstrates select problems for the class. The students are primarily responsible for determining which problems they got correct. How can this activity be adapted to significantly increase rigor?

Before the students come into class, the teacher can post three different homework problems on each of the four walls of the classroom. Those problems will have been intentionally completed incorrectly by the teacher, with all work shown. In four groups, the students should be asked to review the completed problems and determine "why" the problem is incorrect. Then each group will write a paragraph about each problem that explains how the teacher arrived at the incorrect answer and what steps should be taken to correct the problem.

By using this approach, the common process of reviewing homework becomes a rigorous activity in which students have to analyze their teacher's work, compare it to their own homework, and determine the incorrect procedures that were used by the teacher. Some examples will include errors in calculation while other problems, particularly word problems, will include errors in how the teacher approached the problem. This simple activity takes ordinary instruction and turns it into rigorous instruction that will enable students to become sophisticated problem solvers.

This activity also lends itself to differentiation for students who struggle or students with disabilities. On one of the walls, instead of providing a problem that was completed incorrectly, a problem can be completed correctly. Students with disabilities and other students who are struggling with the particular concepts can then be asked to articulate the steps that were conducted in the problem. That way, students use an existing model but must use correct mathematical terminology to explain the steps that occurred. While the other groups are completing their work in small, collaborative groups, the math teacher can work directly with the students who were completing the differentiated problem.

Middle and high school English teachers can also increase their use of rigorous instruction. Students are often asked to read a narrative selection and answer literal and inferential questions in writing. That common activity can be ramped up with rigor. After reading *The Color Purple*, for example, students can be asked to answer comprehension questions in cooperative groups in stations around the room. At each station, students are presented with questions that require them to synthesize the motives, actions, and characteristics of the main characters of the story with present-day activities. For example, the following questions may be placed at each station.

- In the upcoming election, who would Celie vote for? Why?
- There is new legislation that requires small business owners to provide health insurance for their employees. Celie now owns a business that has five employees. Is she in favor of or against this legislation? Why?
- This school district has just established separate schools for boys and girls. Is Celie in favor of or against this initiative? Why?

At each station, the same questions should be asked, but from the perspective of a different character. At one station, identical questions will be asked from the perspective of Mister while at another table the same questions are posed from Shug's perspective. The students must work in their cooperative group to answer the questions at their station, then at a specified time, the students shift to the next station until they have answered three groups of questions. The teacher will then bring all groups together to debrief them on their findings.

The teacher should not allow answers that are too simplistic. For example, students should not be allowed to choose a candidate based on his or her gender, ethnicity, or home state. Students must dig deeper and develop opinions based on deep understandings of the character in the narrative and the current scenarios. This example demonstrates again how routine instructional activities, in this case reading comprehension, can be altered to increase rigor and enable students to become sophisticated learners.

This activity can also be differentiated for students with disabilities and other students who struggle, except this time the differentiation can occur in heterogeneous groups. A list of descriptive words and phrases can be provided at each station that describes the respective character. One character may have descriptors such as "independent," "compassionate," and "thoughtful." The list of words can be used by any member of the group. It will assist students with disabilities and other students who struggle by activating their knowledge about the characters and giving them a starting point for the discussion.

RESEARCH-BASED INSTRUCTIONAL STRATEGIES

GREAT instruction also includes the use of research-based instructional strategies. For far too long, educators have jumped on the latest instructional trend or gimmick. The educational community can be easily swayed by thin research, shiny brochures, quick headlines, or slick salespeople. When educators try to implement research-based instruction, they often rely exclusively on vendors' marketing information. Unfortunately, many vendor catalogs announce that their products are now "research-based" whether or not there is any truth to that statement.

Since the term is bandied about so freely, it makes sense to ask, "What exactly does 'scientifically research-based' mean?" It depends on who you ask. Many educators would say that anything that is published could be described as "research-based." There are many journals and books (this being one) that are published but certainly do not meet the criteria of having been the product of "scientifically based research." These publications (hopefully including this one) can be very useful in helping schools implement effective practices, but they do not warrant the descriptor of "scientifically based research."

The No Child Left Behind legislation (2001) defined the components of "scientifically based research." Among other criteria, the legislation stated that "scientifically based research" includes:

- randomized assignment of participants to various conditions;
- replicable studies;
- reliable and valid data across evaluators and observers, across multiple measurements, and across studies;
- rigorous data analysis that can effectively be used to draw a conclusion;
- systematic, empirical methods;
- objective and systematic procedures that can lead to valid and reliable conclusions.

In essence, the definition of "scientifically based research" provided in the No Child Left Behind legislation describes the type of research that is often seen when a new medicine is being tested. To oversimplify, subjects are randomly assigned to multiple groups. The randomization of the participants, when completed sufficiently, minimizes the impact of the differences, or variables, between the various subjects. The subjects are then provided different interventions and their results are compared.

By using the medical approach, researchers can, to a point, state that the intervention had an impact on the changes in the subjects. The medicine, therefore, can be linked to improved health or a reduction of the symptoms of a particular medical condition. If multiple studies are conducted by various researchers and a particular intervention is connected to groups with better outcomes, then it can be stated that the intervention has "scientifically based research" to support it.

In the educational arena, this type of research can be used to determine whether an instructional strategy has a link to increased learning. A particular reading strategy might be compared to other strategies to determine if it increases reading comprehension, for example. Did multiple research studies reveal that students who received the particular instructional strategy demonstrate more growth in reading comprehension than the comparison groups? If so, then the instructional strategy can be described as being supported with "scientifically based research." This is a very high bar or, as some would say, the "gold standard" of research.

Recommendations of the National Reading Panel

What are some of the scientifically based instructional strategies that should be seen in elementary schools where one of the primary goals is to teach students to become effective readers? According to the National Reading Panel, in 1997, the United States Congress became concerned about the lack of a consensus on effective reading instruction and asked the National Institutes of Health to establish a panel to review the effectiveness of various approaches to teaching reading ("About the National Reading Panel" 2001).

After conducting a significant, although not exhaustive, review of the research in reading that met the standards of "scientifically based research," the panel determined that there are five core components that are beneficial in teaching reading. Those five dimensions of reading include instruction in: phonemic awareness (the ability to recognize and manipulate the sounds in words), phonics, comprehension, fluency (the ability to read smoothly and quickly), and vocabulary. The panel recommended specific instructional strategies for each of these areas. Teachers should analyze students' skills in the five components and provide explicit instruction with research-based strategies to strengthen students' areas of weakness (National Institute of Child Health and Human Development 2000).

National Mathematics Advisory Panel

In 2008, a similar group of experts published a report making recommendations to improve the mathematics achievement of students across the country. The National Mathematics Advisory Panel (2008) made recommendations that would impact the achievement of all students.

For example, all students need mathematics teachers who have a deep understanding of mathematics. Therefore, school districts must ensure that all teachers who provide mathematics instruction, whether they are general education teachers or special education teachers, participate in ongoing training and support that will enable them to become experts in mathematics. Schools must also strive toward hiring math teachers who are experts in their content areas.

The panel also addressed the historical conflict between different camps in math instruction. At various times, different groups have promoted instruction that focuses almost exclusively on problem solving and concept understanding. At other times, the education pendulum has swung in the opposite direction and computational basics have dominated instruction.

The National Mathematics Advisory Panel stressed the importance of all three of these elements. To become high-achieving math students, students need to be able to compute effortlessly and fluently while having strong foundations in concept understanding and sophisticated problem-solving abilities. According to the panel, these elements are mutually important. Classroom instruction should include a balanced approach in which students become proficient in each of the three elements.

The panel also found consistently weak areas of student achievement and instruction in some particular areas. They recognized that many students have fundamental weaknesses in understanding and working with fractions, decimals, and percents. These three related concepts are often not taught efficiently in our nation's classrooms and therefore, many students lack proficiency in understanding, problem solving, and computation in these areas. Unfortunately, introductory instruction in fractions is often limited to concrete representations like using a pizza to demonstrate different parts of a whole (one-half, one-fourth, etc.). Limiting instruction to such a concrete representation is limiting students' sophisticated understanding of fractions.

Students should be taught that a fraction is a number just like any other number and can be represented on a number line. By teaching and practicing with fractions on a number line, students can begin to understand the relationships between fractions and whole numbers. They can understand how different computational procedures impact the quantity of fractions and how different fractions (in proper and improper forms) compare in size.

The panel also noted the importance of reinforcing students' effort in math. Unfortunately, many students (and adults for that matter) think that there are some people who are inherently good at math and then there are others who will not be good at math no matter how hard they try. You hear that in everyday conversations. You might hear someone say, "I'm not a math person. I can't even balance my checkbook."

That type of statement is considered socially acceptable and others often nod in agreement. By contrast, you would never hear someone say, "I'm not good at reading. I can't even get through the newspaper without struggling." It seems to be socially acceptable to be weak at math and yet it would never be desirable to be a nonreader.

We must help students understand that there aren't "math people" and "nonmath people." Effectiveness in math is not an inherent quality that some people have and others don't. Students and adults get better at math by trying hard, receiving effective instruction, and practicing their skills. We must reinforce students for their efforts in mathematics and help them draw connections between their effort and their increasing math skills. We cannot allow students with disabilities and other students who struggle to place artificial limits on themselves because in their own mind they are not "math people."

The National Mathematics Advisory Panel made several recommendations that apply to all students, but they also made specific instructional recommendations for "low achieving students and students with learning disabilities" (48). The panel stated that students with math disabilities need explicit instruction in mathematics. That instruction includes:

- "Teachers explaining and demonstrating specific strategies and allowing students many opportunities to ask and answer questions."
- Students thinking aloud "about the decisions they make while solving problems."

- "Careful sequencing of problems by the teacher or through instructional materials to highlight crucial features."

In addition, the panel also stated that Direct Instruction, a scripted and highly sequenced approach to explicit instruction, yielded positive results. They also stated that some instructional time "should be dedicated to ensuring that students possess the foundational skills and conceptual knowledge necessary for understanding the mathematics they are learning at their grade level" (49).

It is interesting that the panel made the same recommendations for students with disabilities and those who struggle but have not been identified as having a disability. This supports the earlier contention in this book that the instructional strategies that are needed for students with disabilities will also benefit other students who struggle.

Both groups of students often have holes in their learning. Therefore, instruction needs to be implemented that includes an analysis of students' mathematical competencies and, more importantly, where students are missing knowledge and skills. Targeted instruction can then be provided that shores up those holes to equip students to learn grade-level performance standards. Both groups of students will also benefit from explicit instruction in mathematics. In fact, explicit instruction in all subject areas is the cornerstone of effective instruction for students with disabilities.

The "I Do It, We Do It, You Do It" of Explicit Instruction

Students with disabilities and those who struggle but do not have disabilities need explicit instruction. They need the teacher to demonstrate new skills. They need to practice those new skills while receiving guidance and feedback from the teacher. Finally, the students need to practice those skills independently. Anita Archer developed a moniker to describe the pattern of modeling, guided practice, and independent practice—"I do it, we do it, you do it" (Hughes and Archer, in press).

Teachers need to clearly explain and demonstrate the new skills that are expected, let's say writing a persuasive essay. They need to show models of effective persuasive essays, and then actually model prewriting strategies that will lead to drafting. Then the teacher needs to show how those prewriting strategies develop into the actual essay. By showing various examples of completed persuasive essays, students gain a clear understanding of what the final product will look like in various forms. By seeing multiple examples, students can see the commonalities that make each of the examples fit into the category of persuasive essay while seeing different ways in which different authors shared their viewpoint.

As teachers turn toward demonstrating the prewriting strategies and show how those elements are transformed into the final essay, students see the specific process that they should use to complete a persuasive essay. All of this modeling constitutes the "I do it" of explicit instruction.

After the demonstrations are complete, students should be given an opportunity to complete prewriting and writing activities with guided practice. Differentiation can be incorporated in all parts of the instructional process, but it should be clearly evident during the guided practice ("We do it") portion of the lessons. Different students will need different intensities of feedback and targeted guidance. Some students will complete the prewriting and writing activities with less guidance and feedback while other students will need more assistance.

Finally, students complete the activity with little to no support. This "You do it" component of explicit instruction enables the teacher and the student to determine how proficient the student has become. Their efforts can be assessed to determine where instruction must go next.

Depending on their areas of weakness, students with disabilities and other students who struggle need explicit instruction in different subject areas and in different aspects of instruction. Students not only need this type of instruction in the content, but also in the metacognitive strategies that are needed and the specific instructional activity.

In a history class, for example, some students will not only need explicit instruction on the content (the causes of the Great Depression), but they will also need explicit instruction in the process of planning, researching, and writing a research paper (metacognitive strategy) and the various instructional activities that are undertaken in the class (e.g., having a debate in class). Some students, such as high-achieving students, can be successful with mere guidance and facilitation from the teacher, but students with disabilities and other students who struggle need explicit instruction.

Some educators might assume that explicit instruction is the opposite of rigorous instruction. That, in fact, is quite untrue. They may also assume that explicit instruction will dictate that teachers spend the majority of their time in providing lectures to large groups of students. Again, that is untrue. Explicit instruction can be extremely rigorous and can be implemented in a variety of ways to large groups and small, flexible groups of students.

Vocabulary Instruction

It is very beneficial for students with disabilities and other students who struggle to participate in explicit vocabulary instruction. Unfortunately, many people assume that vocabulary development is synonymous with learning specific terminology. That is one aspect of vocabulary development, but the larger context also includes increasing students' expressive and receptive language skills.

All children should demonstrate an ever-increasing skillfulness at reading, writing, and speaking. Students should use and understand a wide variety of terms, but they should also use language (orally and in print) in various ways depending on the context. As students get older, they should be able to express themselves in elaborated and complex ways. They should be able to express subtle and nuanced differences when the situation calls for that. Students should be able to respond with different emphasis (e.g., emotionally) depending on the situation or the material that is presented.

Recent research indicates that all children do not come to school with the same foundation in vocabulary and language. According to Hart and Risley (1995), children from families from different socioeconomic strata have widely different language experiences before coming to school. In an average hour, for example, preschool children from families receiving welfare heard more than 600 words in a typical hour, while the average child from a working-class family heard more than 1,200 words and the average child from a professional family heard more than 2,100 words.

Therefore, the results of the study indicate that children from the highest socioeconomic strata heard almost four times as many words in a typical hour than did their least-advantaged peers. Hour upon hour of this type of discrepancy can have a significant impact on children's language and vocabulary development before they ever enter kindergarten.

Just as some students from economically difficult circumstances face language and vocabulary challenges, many students with disabilities exhibit difficulties. Students with learning disabilities, for example, may face multiple barriers to vocabulary and language development. Students with learning disabilities may have memory and processing problems that interfere with their ability to initially learn vocabulary terminology through everyday experiences or through classroom instruction. Therefore, their ability to add terminology and improve language usage may be weaker than their peers without disabilities.

Just as the diminished exposure to words can have a cumulative impact on children from lower economic circumstances, students with disabilities who have difficulty acquiring new words face cumulative deficits. Many students with disabilities exhibit suppressed language and vocabulary skills or significant holes in their development due to the lower pacing of learning year after year when compared to their peers without disabilities.

It is apparent that vocabulary/language development is critical for all students, but can be especially important for students from economically disadvantaged circumstances and those with disabilities. Many children are in both of those potentially vocabulary-impacting subgroups.

The focus on language also passes the common sense test. Strong students have long since recognized that they have an advantage once they master the terminology, language, and vocabulary of a particular field. Many individuals have figured this out in college. Those individuals who are often labeled as "good students" learned that as soon as they mastered the "lingo" of a particular professor or the terminology in a certain field of study, then they were halfway home in gaining and demonstrating proficiency. In fact, a skillful student can often use terminology effectively (the "buzz" words) and trick the professor into believing they have more proficiency than they actually have. The fact that some students can outwit their professors with well-placed terminology demonstrates the power of vocabulary.

Vocabulary/language development can be considered in two broad ways. First, students need a wide variety of interactions with as much language as possible. They need language-rich environments where they are engaged with using, investigating, playing with, and seeking out new terminology and new uses of words that they already know. Classroom teachers need to emphasize using novel words in speech and in written expression.

Students need practice in investigating new words encountered in discussion and speech. Teachers must create classroom processes and instruction in which children are seeking out, gathering, and experimenting with new terminology. When observing classrooms, observers should routinely see the investigation, manipulation, and interaction with terminology to be ever-present in all classrooms.

In addition to creating the processes and environment described above, students need explicit instruction in particular terminology that is related to the curricular expectations. In fact, since all students in a particular grade/subject will be pursuing the same curricular standards, common vocabulary lists should be created that relate to the standards.

Ideally, the school district should convene a group of experts in the various subject matters who establish vocabulary lists for each grade, content area, and course. The vocabulary terms should not be limited to terminology that is extremely idiosyncratic to a particular field. In addition to those terms, the lists should include words that have a variety of uses and applications, thereby increasing students' vocabulary across contexts.

This approach to specific vocabulary terminology seems to be more reliable than allowing each teacher to individually develop a list of terms related to the curricular standards. The lists can certainly be expanded upon by each teacher, but the core vocabulary terms should be consistent across teachers who teach the same grade/subject. The school or district should also provide curriculum maps that demonstrate in the curriculum where the various vocabulary words should be taught during the instructional year. This information should pinpoint a rough schedule during the year when specific words should be initially addressed. This can be helpful for speech pathologists or other service providers who want to align their therapy with classroom instruction.

Once the timelines and terminology lists are established, explicit vocabulary instruction must be implemented. Unfortunately, vocabulary instruction in many schools and classrooms is limited to providing a list of new words to the students, requiring students to look up the words in the dictionary and rewrite their definitions, and then expecting them to write a sentence with those words. Relying solely on these activities will almost certainly ensure that students will not increase their vocabulary/language skills.

Students need vocabulary activities that enable them to gain understanding of new terminology. They need to hang the new words on existing knowledge and expand that knowledge with the new terms. One explicit vocabulary strategy involves creating categories with terms and then developing categories from those same terms. Let's say that middle school students are studying an instructional unit that includes this partial list of terms: *obsessive, excitedly, subtle, exasperation, sneaky, selected, drafted,* and *determined.*

First, students should place the terms in student-developed groups. At first glance, there may be four different groups of terms. Because of their related meaning, students might pair the following words: (1) *obsessive/determined,* (2) *subtle/sneaky,* (3) *abundant/excessive,* and (4) *selected/drafted.* These terms have similar meanings given a specific context. The students respectively label these groups: (1) extreme focus, (2) not being noticeable, (3) plenty, and (4) chosen.

Some students may develop different groups for these terms, which is not only acceptable but should be encouraged. In fact, student learning is maximized when the students discuss various groupings and provide their rationale for their choices. Their discussions and reworking of the groups deepen both their knowledge and use of the terms.

Next, students should develop categories from the words. This time, each term becomes the title for its own category. Therefore, students have to focus on the differences in the terms rather than their similarities. Under each word, they should write information like: the context in which the term is used, who might use the word, and properties that make the word unique. They can also list related words. For example, under the term *abundant,* a student might write the following phrases:

- Means that there is plenty.
- More than expected.

- It is a good thing.
- Will make people happy.
- Related words and ideas: food, Thanksgiving, time in the summer, and so forth.
- Example: If there was lots of food at a party and everyone was happy.

Under the word *excessive*, a student might write the following phrases:

- Means there is plenty.
- Having too much.
- It is a bad thing.
- Will make people feel uncomfortable.
- Related words and ideas: eating too much and feeling sick, costing too much money, and so forth.
- Example: A person talked too much and people didn't like being around him/her.

Notice that even though these words have similar meanings, their context is very different. One of the terms has a positive connotation while the other term has a negative connotation. Of course, there might be a context in which that does not stay true, but by and large this activity enables students to develop a deeper understanding of the words. These types of activities will also increase the likelihood that the terms will become a part of the students' lexicon.

Teachers should be equipped with a rotation of ten to fifteen vocabulary instructional activities that give the students the opportunity to revisit terms and think about their meanings in a variety of ways. The point here is that students should continually add to their understanding of the terminology by completing activities that help the student view the words through a variety of lenses, situations, and perspectives, thereby creating a deep understanding of the terminology.

In order to increase students' opportunity to revisit words, activities should be provided that are cumulative in nature. At various times of the year, students should "pull out" their comprehensive list of words used throughout the semester or year and complete activities that allow the students to interact with all of their words. This will enable students to connect new terms that they are using to words and phrases that they have learned previously.

Ideally, students should have a vocabulary notebook in each of their classes. That way, vocabulary activities are very natural and routine. Students should be adding terms and their documentation of activities to their vocabulary notebook. They can then use the notebook to revisit their cumulative list and past activities regularly.

Preteaching Vocabulary

Students with disabilities generally need many more turns or opportunities for practice at a given skill to gain proficiency than their nondisabled peers. In addition, students with disabilities may not come to certain terms and subject areas with the same degree of background information or familiarity as their nondisabled peers. Therefore, preteaching vocabulary terminology is an extremely efficient strategy for "preparing the soil" for continued instruction.

Visual Organizers

Visual organizers can also be effective at improving student achievement. They can provide an excellent aid for organizing information. Teachers often lead students as they use word webs, for example, to structure information that they are attempting to learn. At the initial stages of using visual organizers, teachers will often provide the students with a graphic organizer format that will be most helpful given the particular subject matter that is being studied. One type of visual organizer might be used for sequencing information in a history class whereas different visual organizers might be used when the content contains new vocabulary words, and still another to demonstrate cause-and-effect relationships.

Many teachers stop there, which limits the positive impact of using visual organizers. As students become more competent in using visual organizers, teachers should reduce their prompting so that students eventually construct visual organizers that summarize important components of the content and clearly demonstrate and simplify the sometimes complex relationships between the components. A student who is adept at creating and using visual organizers can demonstrate advanced levels of learning, starting with a blank page and unifying information from a variety of sources and contexts to represent a coherent message.

A high school student in a U.S. history class, for example, should be able to synthesize information about the civil rights movement from a variety of sources (textbooks, visiting speakers, research, visual arts, government documents, legislation, etc.) to present recommendations to another country about how to move from a system of inequality in their country toward a system of equity. This visual organizer should pull together recommendations based on accomplishments in the United States, and also help that country avoid ineffective strategies utilized in our country.

The student should be able to develop a visual organizer that is succinct and perhaps idiosyncratic in structure but conveys specific and sometimes complex messages in a clear and concise manner. In addition, the student should be able to explain and defend the content of the visual organizer so that an observer can understand the student's recommendations and the rationale for them. By utilizing visual organizers in this way, teachers will be providing rigorous and complex instruction and students will learn at deep levels.

Most students will not be able to begin using visual organizers in this manner. Teachers will need to introduce organizers in concrete and simple ways. Over time, teachers should eventually move students toward more independent and complex implementation. Ultimately, teachers will enable students to review all of the information that was presented over the past two weeks from a variety of sources and develop a one-page graphic organizer (starting with a blank page) that summarizes the most important components and clearly demonstrates how those components are interrelated.

Visual organizers offer a great opportunity to provide explicit instruction, not only in the content but also in the metacognitive strategy of using visual organizers. The teacher can model the use of simple visual organizers in the "I do it" phase, provide guided support as students begin to use visual organizers ("We do it"), and then pull back as students use (and eventually develop) visual organizers independently ("You do it").

Visual organizers also offer an instructional activity in which differentiation can be provided for students with disabilities and other students who struggle. Teachers can adjust the rate at which select students transition to visual organizers with less support. They can also provide students with disabilities and other struggling students with a choice of three visual organizers to choose from as they develop their own. This way, they have a clear path to develop their thoughts. Eventually, they will be able to produce these three types independently, while not being distracted by all of the potential options that they have when developing their own unique visual organizer.

After creating the visual organizer, every student in the class should be expected to explain the information in their visual organizer. In small groups, the teacher and the rest of the class can determine if the student was able to prioritize important information, exclude less important information, and summarize the relationships between all of the components.

Differentiation can also include the degree to which explicit instruction is provided while preparing students to describe their visual organizers. Teachers may explicitly teach students with disabilities and other students who struggle to start their discussion with the big ideas and then provide supporting details. Other students who do not have disabilities or do not struggle may not need such explicit instruction in making a visual organizer or in describing it.

Middle and High Schools

What about the instructional strategies used in middle and high schools? In too many middle and high schools, two instructional strategies are overused: teacher lecture and student independent work. Many teachers alternate between lecturing students with information and then passing out assignments. (As mentioned previously, they may assume that they are implementing explicit instruction effectively.) There is certainly a place for both of these instructional strategies but in many middle and high school classrooms they dominate the instruction.

In many math classes, for example, the teacher provides examples of math problems on a projector and then gives students assignments to complete independently. In and of itself, this can lead to low levels of learning. Students do need to have specific processes explicitly taught to them. Then they need the opportunity to try those processes out in a variety of contexts. Instead of only completing pages of math problems in geometry classes in high schools, for example, students need the opportunity to construct various structures quickly and determine how the various shapes and sizes intersect to change the structure's area.

Many researchers have recommended specific instructional strategies. Marzano, Pickering, and Pollock (2001), for example, report on their meta-analysis of instructional strategies and recommend nine classroom practices that have a positive impact on student learning. Those strategies are: "identifying similarities and differences," "summarizing and note taking," "reinforcing effort and providing recognition," "homework and practice," "nonlinguistic representations," "cooperative learning," "setting objectives and providing feedback," "generating hypotheses," and "questions, cues, and advance organizers."

Fidelity

Choosing instructional strategies that are grounded in research meets only half of the challenge of teaching effectively. An equally important issue is whether teachers implement those instructional strategies with fidelity. All too often teachers are provided relatively limited opportunities to learn about new strategies through one-day workshops or professional conferences. They then try out those strategies and unknowingly implement them inaccurately.

They may not provide the instruction in the way that the strategies have been designed and studied. They may not provide sufficient intensity of instruction. They may not be implementing the instructional strategies with sufficient frequency, or providing appropriate feedback to students. Teachers must use research-based instructional strategies and implement those strategies with fidelity.

What can a school do to ensure that the research-based strategies that they adopt are implemented with fidelity? A school or perhaps the school district must ensure that they have shared information about how specific strategies should be implemented. This information should be extremely concrete and specific. Teachers should be allowed to layer their own personality and style on the instructional strategy only as long as their implementation is within the parameters of how the instructional strategy has been studied and shown to be effective.

Implementation with fidelity is also impacted by the degree to which ongoing coaching and monitoring are provided. Teachers must be given opportunities to attempt their strategies, receive feedback on the implementation, brainstorm improvements, and refine the strategy implementation over time. These activities must be framed within a context of accountability and monitoring. In addition to providing coaching and support, school leaders must ensure that teachers' strategy implementation is steadily moving toward fidelity.

The Availability of Scientifically Based Research

The amount of "scientifically based research" is very limited, unfortunately, in many academic content areas and in many grade levels. Out of necessity, schools have to rely on instructional strategies that have undergone less strenuous research. The main recommendation here is to have someone on your staff or someone in your school district who is knowledgeable about research-based strategies and can evaluate the claims made by vendors, researchers, or other schools.

This is extremely important as "quick fixes" can be rampant regarding the education of students with disabilities. Virtually every month there is a new claim made about a new instructional strategy, a unique program, or a specialized therapy. There may even be reliable stories that a particular intervention caused tremendous gains for a particular individual with a disability.

That type of progress for students with disabilities is to be admired, but educators should also show a healthy skepticism about cure-all claims. Students with disabilities can actually have setbacks if educators fully implement an intervention that proves to be unsuccessful. Months of instructional time can be wasted on ineffective interventions when that time could have been used more efficiently to assist the student in making progress.

Professionals in your school district who are experts in critiquing research must be given the opportunity to review the research and share their findings in clear, concise, and understandable ways. That way, the educators in your district and school are much less likely to adopt interventions that will not be fruitful. The research experts in your district/school may access information provided by independent entities that review educational research. For example, the What Works Clearinghouse (n.d.) provides objective reviews of research on specific educational and instructional interventions. The clearinghouse was established by the U.S. Department of Education's Institute of Education Sciences to provide educators with reliable information on educational research.

The professionals who review the research should provide concise summaries of the recommendations. Those summaries should include specific descriptions of how the instructional strategies should be implemented in accordance with the research and for which group of students with disabilities. Over time, the school district can adopt specific strategies, based on its own evaluation of the existing research, rather than relying on the claims of vendors or other professionals who have a financial, philosophical, or at the very least, emotional interest in a specific instructional strategy. In many cases, you will choose to support instructional strategies that do not meet the criteria of "scientifically based research," but that does not mean that you should automatically accept anything that is in print.

Educators should be critical consumers in determining if recommendations have objective research to support them. Educators should also enlarge their information networks by asking schools that have implemented interventions and programs about the positive and negative aspects of the particular practices on the achievement of students with disabilities. A little bit of information about the actual implementation and success of initiatives can be quite informative.

When discussing instructional interventions with other schools, attempt to determine if reported improvements in student achievement were caused by the specific instructional interventions. Many schools unwittingly alter other variables that may have had the positive impact.

Several years ago, one school reported that altering the classrooms (dimming the lights, playing soft music, etc.) for the fourth-grade students had an admirable impact on students' reading and math abilities. While describing the interventions, the school administrators stated that they had "put our best teachers in the 4th grade to see if the altered classrooms would have an impact." In this scenario, the improvements in student achievement were probably the result of the pooling of the talented teachers for the fourth grade rather than the changes made to the classroom setting.

SUMMARY

All students with disabilities need GREAT instruction, which includes instruction that is rigorous with research-based strategies. Educational leaders must ensure that all students with disabilities are provided rigorous instruction so that they can make more progress in the allotted time than other students. They must make up ground by not only learning the grade-level curriculum, but they must also fill in the holes in their learning that have developed over time.

Educators must also ensure that students with disabilities become sophisticated problem solvers by having high expectations for those students and by raising the tide of learning for all students. Through the rigorous instruction for all students, and specifically for students with disabilities, many of our students who have traditionally been unsuccessful will become successful.

Educational leaders and teachers must also ensure that research-based instructional strategies are implemented with fidelity. Students with disabilities must have explicit instruction, not only in the content but also in learning strategies and instructional activities. Teachers must implement the explicit instruction process of modeling, guided practice, and independent practice. They must also implement instructional strategies that are recommended by the National Reading Panel and the National Mathematics Advisory Panel.

In addition, teachers must ensure that they implement explicit vocabulary instruction, visual organizers, and other research-based instructional strategies with fidelity. The strategies must be implemented in the way that research has indicated. Teachers should certainly infuse their personality and teaching style into those strategies, but only as long as instructional fidelity is maintained.

Questions for Reflection

1. Are the students with disabilities in your school routinely provided rigorous instruction? Do the school leaders and general education and special education teacher have high expectations and provide instruction that will enable them to become sophisticated learners? Explain your answer.
2. Is rigorous instruction provided routinely across the school for all students? Are teachers primarily teaching students toward the minimum passing score or are they striving for the proverbial "840"? What evidence do you have to support your answer?

3. Do the general education and special education teachers routinely provide explicit instruction with great expertise? Do teachers implement the "I do it, we do it, you do it" steps of explicit instruction in all classes to ensure that students with disabilities and other students who struggle meet high expectations? Provide a rationale for your answer.

4. What specific research-based instructional strategies are used with fidelity across the school? Are the teachers and leaders in your school familiar with research-based instructional strategies and is it obvious that there is great effort to ensure that the strategies are implemented with fidelity?

Chapter Four

Engaging and Exciting

There is another component of GREAT instruction that is critically important but is more difficult to quantify. Students need "magic." They need to be pulled in and engaged in instruction. When you walk in some classrooms, this "magic" is apparent.

You will see it from that magnificent second-grade teacher who waits until his or her students are out of the room to place green construction paper footprints all over the room. When the students line up outside of the room to enter, the teacher looks astonished and says, "You won't believe what happened. A leprechaun visited our room when we were out. His footprints are everywhere. And it looks like he left a story on everyone's desk. I'm not sure we should read the story. What do you think?" (personal communication, L. Eggers, November 15, 1993). Of course the children will say almost in unison "Yes. Let's read the story." The children will be pulled into the instruction. Their eyes will be shining and they will be completely enthralled in their activity.

You can also see this "magic" in middle and high school classrooms. A creative geometry teacher will not rely solely on worksheets to practice determining the area of various shapes. Instead, he or she will give the students the following assignment to solve in cooperative groups: *Build a dog house for a full-grown Sheltie. The height must exceed the width. The doghouse can include a cube but cannot exclusively be a cube. The area of the dog house must be as close to 1,142 cubic units as possible.*

The teacher will then provide the students with a toy like Super Fort, which is made by Cranium. They are essentially noodles typically used as floats in swimming pools except they have magnets on each end. The students can quickly build a structure using these toys. Most importantly, they can easily tinker with the structure until they develop a final product. They will alternate between their mathematical equations and the structure and make adjustments until they have arrived at a reasonable answer for the problem.

The teacher will watch teams become completely engaged in their work and collaborate as they work toward their final goal. Some students will immediately start building while other students will approach the challenge by solving mathematical problems on paper. The skillful teacher will quietly fade into the background to observe the students as they discuss and brainstorm their solutions.

The teacher will facilitate effective problem solving when needed but will allow the students an opportunity to attempt and reattempt various options. The bell can ring and students will not want to abandon their work. This is "magic" and is a combination of teacher competence and enthusiastic, energetic, and engaging delivery of instruction. It is a combination of substance and style.

Student engagement is important for all students but particularly for students with disabilities. While many students with disabilities have been very successful in school, other students with disabilities have years of unsuccessful experiences. Some of those students respond by demonstrating a lack of engagement. If you were to observe a high school mathematics class, for example, and see several students who are disengaged with the activity, there is a good chance that at least some of those students have disabilities.

Therefore, instruction must provide opportunities for students to be engaged and excited by their work. Teachers need to provide a variety of novel experiences that will pull students into their work. All students, but particularly students with disabilities, need magic in their classrooms.

Questions for Reflection

1. Across your school, do you typically see all students fully engaged in their schoolwork? Explain your answer.
2. Across the school, are the students with disabilities routinely engaged in instructional activities? If there is a barrier with engagement, why is that?

Chapter Five

Assessed Continuously to Guide Instruction

Instruction should also be continuously assessed through the use of progress monitoring of student learning. According to O'Connor and Williams (2006), for decades elementary schools have taught spelling in the same manner. On Monday, students receive a new list of spelling words. During the week, they complete a variety of activities, including writing sentences with the words, defining the words, and perhaps playing spelling games. On Friday, the students take a spelling test.

What happens on the following Monday? All students receive a new set of words. In many cases, the results of Friday's spelling test have not been used to impact Monday's spelling words. All students receive the same list. Some students were competent in spelling all of the words before they were even assigned. They received a perfect score on their spelling test. Some students struggled and performed poorly on the spelling test, missing most of the words. Nonetheless, on the following Monday they all receive the same set of new words. The spelling test essentially serves one purpose—to provide a score for the teacher's grade book (O'Connor and Williams, 2006).

The same phenomenon is also seen in high schools. Teachers provide instruction regarding a particular unit for two or three weeks, which is followed by a test or some type of project. The next day, the teacher embarks on the next unit. The teacher does not use the results of the assessment to guide continued instruction. In fact, it often takes the teacher several days or even several weeks to grade the students' tests or projects. Again, the main purpose of the assessment is seemingly to determine a numerical grade for the teacher's grade book.

Teachers should implement progress-monitoring measures to assess the progress of their students in comparison to the curriculum standards. According to L. Fuchs and D. Fuchs (n.d.), one type of progress monitoring is Curriculum Based Measurement (CBM), in which assessments are implemented that compare students' progress over time to the annual expectations of the curriculum. In elementary mathematics, for example, students take an assessment regularly that includes representative problems from the entire year's curriculum on mathematics. This type of CBM includes samples of each of the problem types that the student will see during the year. The specific problems will change, but their complexity throughout the year will remain consistent. Students are asked to answer all of the mathematical problems and their scores are compared over time.

With this approach, school personnel can graph and analyze students' progress compared to the expectations at the end of the year. The progress, or slope, of the number of correct digits in the students' responses is compared to ensure that the student is on course to meet the expectations by the end of the school year. If the student's trend line is sufficiently steep (the percentage of correct digits on the problems) as the year progresses, there is visible evidence that the student is on course for the year-end expectations. As the school year progresses, students will become more proficient in all types of problems and the graphed slope will gradually move upward. L. Fuchs and D. Fuchs (n.d.) state that in reading, spelling, and mathematics, there are more than two hundred empirical studies documenting the positive impact of progress monitoring.

Curriculum Based Measurement is also an effective process for secondary-age students. According to the National Center on Student Progress Monitoring (n.d.), the trend line for students' learning in reading can be charted by having students regularly complete a timed, three-minute maze passage. Their data graphs will demonstrate if their reading skills are progressing sufficiently (their graphed slope is sufficiently steep) to meet the end-of-the-year curricular expectations. Similarly, progress monitoring for written expression can be effectively evaluated with a weekly, timed, five-minute writing sample in response to a prompt. For learning in content areas, progress monitoring can be accomplished by comparing students' responses on timed measures that have the students match vocabulary with their definitions.

Admittedly, the research that is available on Curriculum Based Measures is more substantial for students in early elementary school than for older students. In some instances, schools are developing common assessments that are developed and used by all of the teachers who teach the same grade/subject throughout the school (or course in high school). These common assessments are developed at the school or district level, rather than by individual teachers, to ensure that the assessments are aligned and adequately reflect the complexity of the curriculum.

Whichever approach is used, the progress-monitoring measures should be reliable predictors of how students will perform on the annual assessments. If students are not on course to meet those expectations, then the teachers can analyze the assessment data and use it to adjust instruction to better meet the students' learning needs.

As teachers analyze their progress-monitoring data for individual students and across their class, they should ask, "Are there specific students who are struggling in my class? What needs to be re-taught and how should I re-teach that information? Are there specific students who are exceeding expectations? Are there trends across the class, either positive or negative? If so, what information does that provide about the instruction that was provided on those particular components and how does instruction need to be impacted as our class moves forward?"

Progress monitoring is important for all students, especially students with disabilities and other students who struggle. Since many students with disabilities are behind their peers without disabilities and lag behind the academic expectations for their grade level, instruction must be extremely efficient. There is no time to waste. Students with disabilities must make more progress than their peers without disabilities in the same amount of time in order to reach the end goal of meeting or exceeding expectations on the annual statewide assessments.

At the first sign that students with disabilities are not learning at the expected rate, teachers can adjust instruction to improve student learning. By using sensitive, ongoing assessments, teachers can make adjustments before gaps widen and students get further and further behind.

This approach to measuring the ongoing progress of students with disabilities is somewhat different than what has traditionally been in place. Students with disabilities may have participated in classroom assessments routinely and standardized assessments either annually or less often than that. But in many schools there wasn't an urgency to ensure that students with disabilities were not falling behind. In fact, it was somewhat expected that students with disabilities would fall well behind their peers without disabilities.

By using progress-monitoring data, teachers can respond quickly and increase the learning curve of their students. They do not have to wait until the end-of-the-year assessments to see how they compare to the curriculum standards. They can continually monitor students' progress and tinker with instruction until every student's learning is maximized and their valuable instructional time is as efficient and beneficial as possible.

Questions for Reflection

1. In your school, are there common assessments used that all teachers give in order to determine students' progress toward the standards? If so, what are those assessments? Do teachers systematically analyze the data to determine student progress? Are teachers proficient at analyzing the data to determine students' strengths and weaknesses?

2. In addition to specified data sources across the school, do teachers analyze classroom work (e.g., chapter tests, written assignments) systematically to determine how students are performing in comparison to the standards? Are teachers proficient at analyzing these less formal work samples to determine student progress?

3. Across the school, are teachers altering subsequent instruction based on the analysis of the ongoing data? What evidence do you have that the data is ultimately used to actually alter continued instruction?

Chapter Six

Tailored through Flexible Groups

Assessment to guide instruction, the "A" in GREAT instruction, leads to the next component that should be seen in every classroom—differentiating or tailoring instruction through flexible groups. This element is most often seen in the classrooms of powerful kindergarten and first-grade teachers. When you observe an outstanding primary teacher, you will see students broken into various groups. The teacher utilizes a kidney-shaped table in the back of the room to provide instruction to one group of students while two other groups of students conduct meaningful, independent activities.

If you ask the strong teacher why the students are grouped as they are, the answer will be something like, "This group needs assistance with decoding consonant-vowel-consonant words while that group needs assistance with their sight words." The teacher will then follow up with, "If you come back in a few weeks, you will see a different grouping pattern. I will shuffle the students as I continue to analyze their needs."

The reason that kindergarten and first-grade teachers utilize small-group instruction so frequently is because of their need to ensure that every child is making sufficient progress. The teachers must ensure that young students are building the reading and math basics that will be the foundation for the entire school career. They need to hear each individual child read frequently so they can determine if each student is learning the foundational skills of initial reading.

There is no other way to ensure that typical children are learning to decode than to hear each child read. The structure of the small-group activities enables the teachers to implement progress-monitoring activities by watching students complete math skills and hearing them read. Then the teachers use that information to differentiate and revise instruction in those groups.

Unfortunately, as students get older fewer teachers use flexible groups in order to conduct progress-monitoring activities and then to differentiate instruction. As mentioned earlier, middle and high school instruction is often limited to the teacher lecturing from the front of the room and then giving the students independent assignments. All teachers should provide small-group instruction to monitor students' progress and to differentiate instruction.

Instruction in virtually every class, kindergarten through high school, should involve a combination of large-group and small-group instruction that targets specific needs for the students in the groups. An observer should routinely see students placed in a variety of small groups, and the teacher should be able to explain the rationale for the groupings when asked. The expected response should be something like, "Those three students are having difficulty summarizing information from a technical text. Two students with them are very strong in that skill and needed additional challenges. Those two students are providing tutorial services to those three students a few minutes every day until they acquire those skills."

Using flexible groups is admittedly only one way to provide differentiation for students with various needs. A variety of instructional components can be differentiated. The way information is presented can be varied. The student activity can be customized and the type of work that students complete to demonstrate their proficiency can be altered depending on the needs of the students.

Utilizing flexible groups and facilitating discussion with the teachers about their rationale for those groups create a context in which improvements in differentiation can become concrete. Therefore, flexible grouping is recommended as the priority method for differentiating instruction. It will set the context in which teachers can differentiate instruction in systematic and purposeful ways.

Teachers should have a specific rationale for the grouping patterns. At times, they will utilize homogeneous groups in which all students in a particular group need similar instruction. At other times, teachers will utilize heterogeneous grouping patterns in which students have different instructional needs that can be met in the same group.

As groups are established based on progress-monitoring data, they may take the form of cooperative learning groups, especially as students move toward upper elementary, middle, and high school. If used effectively, cooperative groups can increase student achievement. Unfortunately, these groups are often implemented poorly. In many classes, teachers will separate students into small groups for a quick activity or for an assignment. When provided this scenario, the students often break apart the task and give the various members of the group specific components. Later, they combine their various components into a whole.

The problem with this type of jigsawing is that none of the students gets a comprehensive understanding of the activity. Every student has a small portion of the whole, rather than an entire understanding. When using jigsawing, teachers should make sure that the information is not so broken up that none of the students understands the material in a deep and complex way.

This activity can be especially bothersome for students with disabilities. Many students with disabilities have difficulty making connections between new knowledge and existing knowledge. Because of this problem, many students with disabilities cannot "hang" their new information in the correct, existing "file" in their memory systems. They don't access existing knowledge that sets a context for the new information.

This creates a challenge in accessing the new information when it is needed. Since many students with disabilities have trouble placing their new knowledge in appropriate contexts in their memory, they then have trouble retrieving the information when it is needed. They can't "re-open" the appropriate file to access the new information. Year after year, many students with disabilities have a disorganized method of accessing related information to set a context for new information, and then have difficulty accessing that information when it should be efficiently stored and retrieved.

To continue the metaphor of a filing system, high-performing students have an effective filing cabinet in which information is placed into certain files and related files are connected. Many students with disabilities have a filing system in which information on one topic may be spread out in bits and pieces in unrelated files. For some students with disabilities, the organizational system is so disrupted, it is as if all of the files from the cabinet have been opened and thrown into one large pile. There is no system for storing and accessing information in an efficient way.

Therefore, jigsawing activities create a challenge for many students with disabilities. Jigsawing activities are only successful for students who can take summaries provided by others and develop an organized memory system so that they all fit together and then are placed in appropriate context in their memory for retrieval later on. Many, if not most, students with disabilities will face challenges when the context is not explicitly built or accessed for them. The truth is that jigsawing and other similar activities are not only difficult for students with disabilities. These types of activities also present problems for other students who struggle but do not have a disability label.

Teachers need to ensure that background knowledge and contexts are appropriately accessed before teachers build new knowledge. This can be done very simply. Before providing new information, teachers must explicitly discuss the connections to previous discussions or provide activities that enable students to make the connections themselves. By spending a small amount of time accessing that information, students with disabilities will be much more successful in "setting" their new information.

Cooperative groups can also be implemented poorly in another way. This problem is seen in classes from primary schools through graduate schools of education. When the teacher (or in the case of graduate schools of education, the professor) separates the class into small groups and gives them a series of questions or challenges to solve, one or two of the participants naturally dominate the conversation. These individuals are typically the students who have a natural knack for the subject matter at hand and feel comfortable leading a peer group.

The students with disabilities in the group either fade quickly into the background or they become disruptive because the activity is not meeting their needs. At the end of the cooperative group discussion, the teacher asks the group to select their speaker who will summarize the discussions of the "group."

The individuals who dominated the discussion are typically nominated by their group to share the thoughts of the group, which in actuality are the thoughts of one or two individuals. In these cases, all of the students do not master the concepts. One or two of the students are making progress, but the other students, including students with disabilities, have not been engaged in or understood the work.

There is an easy way to overcome this problem. When the students are originally given the problems or questions to solve, the teacher should inform the class that the person who summarizes the group's discussions will be selected by the teacher when the cooperative activity is completed. This person will not be chosen until the cooperative activity is completed.

This encourages two desirable outcomes. First, all of the students will become engaged in the cooperative group discussions because any of the individuals may be called to represent their group. In addition, the students will feel responsible for preparing each other for the debriefing. This feeling of mutual responsibility benefits the students with disabilities. The teacher will hear the students make statements to each other like, "Ask me the questions to make sure I answer them correctly."

Teachers will see the leaders of the group developing strategies that will help their struggling peers. They may list the answers to the questions in a visual organizer so the students understand the answer. They may highlight the important terms. They become teachers within their group, which not only assists the struggling students but forces the higher-performing students to use higher-order thinking skills to prepare their classmates.

PREPARING FOR INSTRUCTION USING FLEXIBLE GROUPS

For flexible grouping to be implemented effectively, teachers must plan their units and their lessons differently. Teachers can only provide instruction to a small group of students if the other students are engaged in meaningful, independent activities at that same time.

Again, we can look toward effective kindergarten and first-grade teachers for inspiration. As they plan their instructional units, they specifically plan independent activities that can be completed without direct teacher intervention, are engaging, and are meaningfully tied to the curricular standards. Effective kindergarten and first-grade teachers do not provide "busy" work or activities that are not engaging for the students.

During the planning stages, these teachers explicitly plan a list of activities that must be completed with their direct supervision. They also develop a list of activities that can be completed at various centers around the room and that can be completed in small groups or independently. Once rituals and routines are in place, students move smoothly from center to center completing a wide variety of activities, some of which are teacher-led and others which can be completed without that supervision.

Teachers of older students must also do the same thing. As instructional units are being planned, an array of activities must be developed, some of which will require instruction from the teacher and other activities that can be completed with less supervision.

Many middle and high school teachers will state that their students cannot be trusted to complete independent activities. If the rituals and routines are well-established, almost any group of students can participate in activities without immediate teacher attention. If a group of six-year-old students can do it, then certainly a group of older students can do it. The teacher certainly needs to have "eyes in the back of her or his head" to ensure that everyone is on task, but it can be done nonetheless.

SUMMARY

GREAT instruction is tailored through the use of flexible groups, the most concrete and efficient way to differentiate instruction. In this context, teachers can learn the specific needs of students in their class and provide differentiated and targeted feedback to students according to their needs. Implementation is the key. Teachers must ensure that small-group activities are designed so that all students, including students with disabilities, are engaged in meaningful activities that move them toward the academic standards. Those meaningful activities must be available in teacher-led groups as well as in activities that are not directly led by the teacher.

SUMMARY OF GREAT INSTRUCTION

All students should participate in GREAT instruction. Students with disabilities need it. Extremely gifted students may not reach their potential without GREAT instruction, but they may have a shot of reaching the curricular standards without maximized instruction. Students with disabilities need each element of GREAT instruction if they are to meet the curricular standards. GREAT instruction must be:

- **G**uided by the curriculum
- **R**igorous with **r**esearch-based strategies
- **E**ngaging and exciting
- **A**ssessed continuously to guide instruction
- **T**ailored through flexible groups.

Questions for Reflection

1. In your school, what percentage of teachers regularly implement flexible small-group instruction? Why do you think the other teachers do not implement instruction in this way?
2. When you observe small-group instruction, are the students with disabilities fully engaged in the instructional activities? When the answer is yes, what are teachers doing to make that happen? When the answer is no, why do you think that is?
3. When small-group instruction is being implemented successfully in your school, what are the factors that make it successful?
4. When small-group instruction is being implemented unsuccessfully in your school, what are the factors that make it unsuccessful?

Chapter Seven

Including More Students with Disabilities in General Education Classes

In addition to providing GREAT instruction in every classroom, what else can we do to increase the academic achievement of students with disabilities? In many cases, we need to increase the percentage of students with disabilities who receive their instruction in general education classes for a larger portion of the school day. Doesn't it make sense that if we move toward providing GREAT instruction in general education classes, then more students with disabilities can be successful in those settings?

As mentioned previously, the U.S. Department of Education (2005) reports that approximately half of all students with disabilities spend at least 80 percent of their school day in general education classes. In those schools that have a six-segment school day, those students with disabilities spend at least five of those segments in general education classes.

The state of Georgia has a compelling story to tell about educating more students with disabilities in general education classes. In 2000, only 35 percent of students with disabilities across Georgia were spending at least 80 percent of their school day in general education classes, which was far below the national average. In fact, when compared to all of the states across the country, Georgia ranked second from the bottom in the percentage of students with disabilities who spent at least 80 percent of their school day in general education classes (Bryar, O'Connor, O'Connell et al. 2005).

Under the direction of the Georgia Department of Education's Phil Pickens and Marlene Bryar, the director and associate director for the Division for Exceptional Students at that time, Georgia set a priority for increasing the "inclusion" of students with disabilities across the state.

By 2007, the state of Georgia had made stunning progress. According to the Georgia Department of Education, 60 percent of students with disabilities spent at least 80 percent of their school day in general education classes

(Georgia Department of Education 2008a). Georgia went from being the second from the bottom across the country to being well above the national average.

This movement toward "inclusion" made sense considering the context of the passage of the No Child Left Behind legislation. The overwhelming majority of students with disabilities were now being held to the same academic standards as their nondisabled peers. They had to take the same assessments as other students and earn the same score to "meet" the standards. If students with disabilities were going to be tested just like their nondisabled peers and kept to the same standard, school leaders quickly realized that students with disabilities should be exposed to the same instruction that was provided to their peers without disabilities.

Many students with disabilities had a much higher chance of getting instruction in the curricular standards in general education classes than in special education "pull-out" classes. What does this do for student achievement? Do students with disabilities perform at higher levels when they are educated in general education classes with their nondisabled peers? Do students of similar abilities and disabilities who are educated in general education classes perform higher academically than a comparison group of students with disabilities who are educated in pull-out special education classes?

Unfortunately, there aren't concrete answers to those questions. As we mentioned earlier, scientifically based research would need to be conducted to answer that question. Students with disabilities would need to be randomly assigned to general education or special education classes and their progress would have to be compared to determine if their educational placement impacted their achievement.

That type of study is impossible in the United States. According to the IDEA 2004 legislation and all of its prior legislative versions, every student with a disability must be educated in the "Least Restrictive Environment" for that child, which means that each child must be educated "to the maximum extent appropriate with his/her non-disabled peers."

Every year, a group of individuals including school personnel and the student's parent develop the student's Individualized Education Program (IEP). As they develop the student's plan, they must provide educational services in general education classes unless the student cannot be appropriately educated in those settings. In fact, if the IEP team determines that the student should be educated in pull-out classrooms (for any part of the day), then the team must document why that instruction cannot be provided in general education classrooms.

Therefore, at least once a year, the adults who know the student the best (and the student himself once he or she becomes sixteen years old) brainstorm how to educate the student in general education settings if at all possible. Based on this law, it would be illegal to randomly assign students with disabilities to control and experimental groups to conduct a scientifically based study on the impact of different educational placements.

So without the results of scientifically based research, we have to look at evidence that is less stringent to determine if it appears that students are performing at higher levels when they spend more time in general education classes.

The Georgia Department of Education attempted to review the data across the state to answer the question. Across the state, there are 180 traditional school districts (not including special entities like the Department of Juvenile Justice and state-approved charter schools, which count as school districts themselves). According to Bryar (2006), forty-one school districts across the state educated more than 70 percent of their students with disabilities in general education classes for more than 80 percent of the school day. This placement percentage placed those school districts well above the state placement data during that year. Of those forty-one school districts, thirty-three made Adequate Yearly Progress (AYP) at the district level for their disability subgroup, which means that 80 percent of those districts made AYP for the disability subgroup—a percentage that was higher than the other school districts across the state.

Were the inclusive practices in those school districts the reason why they had a higher rate of making AYP when compared to other school districts? The truth is that we do not know. There may have been other variables that played a part in the school districts' success. But there is a good chance that the movement toward inclusive practices is one component contributing to higher student achievement.

Additional evidence can be seen in a large, urban school district in the southeastern region of the United States that we will call the Lake Shore County School System. Lake Shore has a total enrollment of approximately 100,000 students with approximately 9,400 of those students being identified as having disabilities. From 2001 to 2006, Lake Shore County educated between 40 and 42 percent of their students with disabilities in general education classes for more than 80 percent of the school day. By 2006, this inclusive rate was well below the inclusive rate across the state and across the country. After intensive and ongoing training across the school district on including more students with disabilities in general education classes and improving instruction, the percentage of students with disabilities in general education classes during the 2007–2008 school year increased to 49 percent, an increase of approximately 700 students with disabilities across the district.

In addition to this increase, there was a decrease in the percentage of students with disabilities who spent most of their school day in pull-out special education classes. From 2004 to 2006, approximately 28 to 29 percent of the students with disabilities across Lake Shore spent more than 60 percent of their school day in pull-out special education classes. Therefore, they spent more than half of their instructional day segregated from the general education classroom. During the 2007–2008 school year, that percentage dropped to 20 percent, a drop of 8 percentage points from the previous year.

Therefore, in the course of a year, at least 1,450 students spent more time in general education classes than they had the previous year. This movement reflected a tremendous amount of work from principals, assistant principals, lead teachers for special education, general education teachers, special education teachers, and central office staff. The real question, however, is: Did this movement have a positive impact on student achievement?

Under the provisions of the No Child Left Behind legislation, every school must work toward making AYP. All of the student scores are then uploaded to the district level because the school district must also move toward making AYP. In Lake Shore, there are four academic indicators when determining AYP. Elementary and middle school scores are combined to have two sets of scores—math and English/language arts for third through eighth graders. In addition, there are two sets of scores for high school—math and English/language arts—based on the scores of eleventh graders on the graduation test.

During the 2005–2006 school year and the 2006–2007 school year, when a lower percentage of students with disabilities were educated in general education classes, the Lake Shore County School System did not make AYP in any of the four academic areas for students with disabilities. Over a two-year period, the disability subgroup was zero for eight. After the increase in inclusion practices during the 2007–2008 school year, the district made AYP for the disability subgroup in three out of four academic areas, a significant improvement from the two previous years.

During the 2008–2009 school year, the improvements continued. Fifty-three percent of students with disabilities were educated in general education classes for more than 80 percent of the school day, another increase from

Table 7.1. Lake Shore School System—Did the Disability Subgroup Make AYP?

Year	ELA 3rd–8th	Math 3rd–8th	ELA High School	Math High School
2005–2006	No	No	No	No
2006–2007	No	No	No	No
2007–2008	Yes	Yes	Yes	No

the previous year. During that fall, eleventh graders from across the district participated in the high school writing test, a requirement to earn a general education diploma. During the previous year, 45 percent of students with disabilities passed the writing test on their first attempt. During the fall of 2008, 69 percent of students with disabilities passed the test on the first try, an increase of 24 percentage points.

Later in the same school year, additional data suggested that progress was being made. Every year across the state, eleventh-grade students participate in the high school graduation test in four subject areas: English/language arts, math, science, and social studies. The results of those assessments on the eleventh-grade students in Lake Shore School System showed significant improvement when compared to the state's disability subgroup.

- The percentage of students with disabilities who passed the English/language arts section of the graduation test increased from 41 percent in 2008 to 48 percent this year. By comparison, the passing rate for the state's disability subgroup decreased by one point in the same year.
- In 2008, 38 percent of the students with disabilities from Lake Shore passed the math portion of the graduation test. In 2009, 50 percent of the students with disabilities passed this section — a jump of 12 percentage points. The state's disability subgroup increased by 4 percentage points during that same time period.
- In science, 40 percent of the students with disabilities from Lake Shore passed the test, which is an increase of 5 percentage points from the previous year. The state's disability subgroup made a 3-point gain.
- In social studies, the Lake Shore disability group increased from 36 percent of the students passing the test to 46 percent passing. During that same time, the state's disability subgroup increased by 3 points.

The original question was: Does including more students with disabilities in general education classes increase student achievement? The answer is maybe. Once again, we can not tease out the variables that are contributing to students' increased success. In the Lake Shore County School System, a variety of instructional initiatives were put in place across the school district to increase student achievement. Therefore, it is impossible to conclude cause-and-effect relationships reliably.

In my opinion, however, the inclusive practices were one critical component that contributed to the increased achievement of students with disabilities. As more students with disabilities were included in general education classes, those students were given the opportunity to benefit from instructional initiatives and improvements occurring in general education classes.

Those students were caught up in the positive momentum occurring across the district for all students.

Two things typically occur when students with disabilities spend more time in general education classes. First, they receive instruction in the curricular standards. A third grader receives instruction in the standards that are tested of all third graders. Second, there are usually higher expectations. The general education teachers are so accustomed to grade-level expectations that those expectations expand to their students with disabilities. Even though these elements are certainly not universal, they typically occur in general education classes.

This is becoming much more common in schools and school districts across the country. As schools and districts are educating more students with disabilities in general education classes, improvements are being seen for the disability subgroup. The truth, however, is that an environment in and of itself does not improve student achievement.

There is nothing magical about the four walls of the general education classroom or the classmates or the teacher (other than the two things that typically occur in general education classes). Those successful schools and districts are also improving the instruction that is occurring in general education classes. GREAT instruction must occur if we, as educators, are going to maximize the achievement of students with disabilities.

CO-TEACHING OR SHARED TEACHING

One way to successfully educate students with disabilities in general education classes is to provide co-teaching scenarios in which a general education and a special education teacher share teaching duties for a class of students that includes both students with and without disabilities.

According to Burrello, Burrello, and Friend (1996), there are six models of special education/general education co-teaching that describe the configuration of the adults and students in the shared classroom. Those models are: "Team Teaching," "One Teach/One Observe," "One Teach/One Circulate," "Station Teaching," "Alternative Teaching," and "Parallel Teaching."

The first three describe when whole-group instruction is being provided to all of the students. The latter three models describe configurations in which the students are placed in flexible groups with each teacher leading one of the groups. In "Station Teaching," there are at least three groups of students around the room in which students are completing different instructional activities. One teacher supervises one of the groups while the other teacher supervises the second group. The third student group includes independent student activities. The students rotate between the various groups to complete all of the activities.

"Parallel Teaching" describes when the class is divided into two groups. Each teacher leads one of the groups and covers the same instructional material. "Alternative Teaching" describes the scenario in which one teacher leads a larger group of students and the other teacher supervises a smaller group of students. The students in the smaller group may include students who need targeted instruction like preteaching or remediation. Or the group may include students who need additional challenges and rigor.

Villa, Thousand, and Niven (2004) describe similar general education/special education co-teaching configurations using different terminology: "Supportive Teaching," "Parallel Teaching," "Complementary Teaching," and "Team Teaching." Again, some of these models represent whole-group instruction while "Parallel Teaching" represents different approaches to dividing the students into small groups with each teacher supporting a different group.

There are two critical points regarding co-teaching classes. First, both teachers should be actively teaching the entire instructional period. That way, the "teaching time" in one sixty-minute instructional segment can be doubled to 120 minutes of instruction. (This certainly does not mean that the teachers are lecturing. Teaching involves much more than lecturing.)

If it is obvious that one of the adults is dominating the instruction while the other adult merely drifts around the room and reminds students to stay on task, then the real benefit from the shared teacher arrangement will be lost. In co-teaching arrangements, any observer should see both teachers actively engaged in providing instruction and feedback to students.

This is also the ideal time to provide flexible, small-group instruction. Some may argue that one beneficial model is when the two teachers collaborate to lead a whole group of students and, by virtue of their background and expertise, provide well-rounded discussions. I suggest that the real benefit comes when both teachers are responsible for leading a small group of students.

There is a concept that is almost irrefutable in the field of education. Students learn more quickly and more solidly when they are provided more practice opportunities (more "turns") and more feedback when they attempt those turns.

Small-group instruction, when there are two adults in the room, provides an outstanding opportunity to provide that type of intensive practice and feedback.

With a lower student to teacher ratio, each child in one teacher's small group will have the opportunity to have more attempts at practice (e.g., answering the teacher's question, reading a passage, or answering a mathematics problem) and to receive targeted feedback based on their attempt.

The lower student-to-teacher ratio also allows for tailored and differentiated instruction.

The grouping patterns of students with shared teachers follow the same principles as when there is only one adult in the room. The formation of groups should be based on ongoing, formative data. At times the groups will be homogeneous while at other times heterogeneous groups will be implemented. In the two-teacher classroom, care should be taken to ensure that students are not segregated into groups based on a particular categorization. There should not be groups solely composed of students with disabilities or students who are English language learners, for example. Occasionally, in certain contexts, groups may be based on students' interests as well.

Even though the descriptions of co-teaching models provided above describe the pairing of a general education teacher and a special education teacher, the same principles apply anytime there are two adults in a classroom. In many kindergarten classes, for example, there is a kindergarten teacher and a paraprofessional. At other times, there are specialized teachers who coteach in general education classes. A teacher of English language learners may partner with a seventh-grade social studies teacher to serve both students who are proficient in English and students whose primary language is not English.

Regardless of the title or position of the two adults in the room, the real "bang for the buck" occurs when students are split into small instructional groups and each adult provides targeted instruction to different groups. Students have more turns and receive more targeted feedback on their attempts. Because of the lower student-to-teacher ratio, the instruction is much more likely to be differentiated.

As you might have noticed, the emphasis on small-group instruction is aligned with the last element, the "T," of GREAT instruction. Co-teaching scenarios creates a perfect opportunity for teachers to tailor effective small-group instruction. In fact, small-group instruction becomes much more manageable when there are two adults in the room.

FILLING-THE-GAPS INSTRUCTION

In reading, written expression, and mathematics, all students must learn to complete basic skills fluently, without much effort, in order to be competent in higher-order activities. In reading, for example, students must be able to read words fluently in order to comprehend grade-level text. When students have to focus on decoding words in their text, they cannot devote their cognitive energy to understanding the material. Their effort is devoted to figuring out the words rather than determining the message of those words.

In written expression, students must have the ability to write individual sentences and paragraphs fluently. With these fundamental skills, they will be able to tackle more difficult assignments such as writing persuasive essays, developing narratives, and constructing expository compositions. If they stumble on basic writing skills, then they will be unable to demonstrate competence in more complex written expression tasks.

The same barriers exist for students who have not mastered computational skills. Students must be able to complete computational skills automatically so that they can devote their cognitive energy to problem solving. Students will be unsuccessful in solving complex math problems if they have to labor through every computational step.

If students are to become proficient in grade-level reading, written expression, and math skills, they must have strong basic skills. Unfortunately, many students with disabilities have holes in their learning. A sixth-grade student with a disability may have difficulty with decoding in reading, fluent writing, or basic computation. Therefore, some time in the instructional day must be devoted to filling in those holes of learning for many students with disabilities. Unfortunately, most schools are unsuccessful at catching students up once they have fallen behind.

The reason public schools have been unsuccessful in filling students' holes of learning is that we have approached the task with great inefficiency. Traditionally, many schools removed students with disabilities from grade-level instruction and taught them at a lower grade level until they caught up. Many students with disabilities never caught up and were essentially rarely given the opportunity to learn grade-level curriculum.

In the new context of higher expectations and accountability for students with disabilities, we must do both. We must provide students with grade-level instruction in the content areas and also provide extremely intensive instruction in their weak areas to plug the holes in their learning.

Filling-the-Gaps Instruction in General Education Classes

This type of intensive filling-the-gaps instruction can be provided in a variety of contexts. It can be conducted in general education classes. Earlier in the book, it was stated that educators must maximize instructional time for students with disabilities so that students have the opportunity to cover more ground (thereby catching up to their peers) during every instructional period. All students, but particularly students with disabilities, must have meaningful work waiting for them when they enter the classroom. We must also reduce any instructional downtime in our classrooms.

In the general education classroom, opportunities can be provided for students to work on fundamental reading, math, and written expression skills during every moment that has traditionally been wasted instructional time. When entering the room, a variety of instructional tasks, such as repeated oral readings with a partner, quick writing assignments, or practice with computational skills, can be provided. These activities may be limited to ten minutes in each period, but can be extremely powerful in providing intensive instruction and practice for the students.

Earlier in the book, station teaching was also reviewed as an effective way to provide flexible, small-group instruction (when there are one or two adults in the classroom). Stations should be developed in which students are given the opportunity to work on those gaps in their learning. Peer tutors can be used or activities can be developed so that students self-check and correct their work.

This filling-the-gaps instruction will not only benefit students with disabilities but will also prove beneficial to other students who struggle. There are many nondisabled students who have gaps in their learning that are interfering with their success in school.

Filling-the-Gaps Instruction during Double Dosing

In many schools, there is an opportunity to conduct this type of instruction during "double dosing" instructional periods. In many schools, students who are experiencing difficulty in English/language arts or math have the opportunity to participate in an extra period of instruction in that content area. This opportunity is not only afforded to students with disabilities, but is available to all students who struggle in that content area.

Unfortunately, in many schools that period of extra instruction is essentially the same type of instruction that the students received in their first instructional period. The instruction does not change. Students just receive additional time in the subject area, not more targeted instruction. Instruction during those segments should be extremely targeted, intensive, and efficient. In order to make that happen, students must be evaluated to determine the specific holes in their learning.

In mathematics, for example, are students having difficulty with addition, subtraction, multiplication, or division? If students are having difficulty with subtraction, is it single-digit subtraction, subtraction with regrouping, or the conceptual understanding of subtraction?

Once the particular area of weakness is known, then teachers can provide extremely targeted instruction in that area. The instruction should provide students with the opportunity to practice those skills repetitively and receive increased feedback. They will need lots of practice and intensive and directed feedback. Teachers need to ensure that students do not practice those skills incorrectly and therefore compound their misunderstanding.

This type of instruction needs to be short term. When those holes are filled, this portion of the day needs to be used for other instruction. The compensatory instruction does not need to be endless. It needs to be short term. It needs to serve a purpose in filling gaps in learning and then be completed.

Filling-the-Gaps Instruction in Pull-Out Classes

For some students with disabilities, filling-the-gaps instruction will occur during pull-out instruction in a special education setting. This instruction must be carried out with great expertise and a sense of urgency and focus so that students make up for lost ground. Most importantly, this instruction occurs in addition to the grade-level instruction that is occurring during the rest of the school day. The overwhelming majority of students with disabilities should always be pursuing grade-level performance standards.

Filling-the-Gaps Instruction Using Technology

Over the past several years, software has been developed in which individualized instructional activities are provided. The software provides an assessment in order to determine the specific gaps in a student's skills. Then a series of activities is provided that tailor to that student's needs. When students answer questions correctly, they are provided more difficult problems. When they show patterns of weaknesses, specific computerized instruction is provided to remediate the student's gaps. This is another alternative in providing targeted, fill-the-gaps instruction in both general education and special education settings for students with disabilities.

Questions for Reflection

1. In your school, do most students with disabilities spend at least 80 percent of their school day in general education classes?

2. Are there opportunities to include more students with disabilities in general education classes for a larger portion of the school day? Specifically, which students with disabilities in your school should spend more time in general education classes and for what classes?

3. In your school's co-teaching classes, what type of co-teaching do you see? Are the preferred models of co-teaching used the majority of the time? The preferred co-teaching models are evident when students are split into multiple small groups with targeted instruction with each teacher leading a different group of students.

4. Is filling-the-gaps instruction provided in general education classes for all students, but specifically for students with disabilities who have holes in their learning? Are these instructional activities effective? Explain your answer.

5. Does your school use double dosing for students with and without disabilities who are struggling in a particular academic area? Describe the instruction that is provided in those classes. Is the double dosing merely more time in the subject area or is instruction provided that is targeted and efficient to close students' particular learning holes? Describe how students' specific areas of weaknesses are determined and how teachers provided targeted instruction in those areas for particular students.

6. In pull-out special education classes, is filling-the-gaps instruction provided with great intensity, accuracy, and urgency? Are students who are participating in that type of instruction succeeding at filling their academic holes?

Chapter Eight

Behavioral Challenges

Some students with disabilities experience behavioral challenges that interfere with their ability to be successful in school. The behavioral challenges may also interfere with the instruction that is provided to other students. What interventions should be put in place when students exhibit behavioral difficulties that interrupt learning? There are different layers of answers to this question.

ENSURE GREAT INSTRUCTION IS PROVIDED ROUTINELY

What is the opposite of misbehavior? Many people incorrectly believe that "behaving" is the antithesis to misbehavior. That is false. The opposite of misbehavior is engagement. Many students exhibit negative behavior because they are not routinely engaged in meaningful instructional activities. In particular teachers' classrooms, they may be tired of instructional activities that lack excitement, are too repetitive, or seem to be meaningless. They exhibit inappropriate behavior to create some excitement or to respond to activities that seem to be going nowhere.

The first antidote for misbehavior is to ensure that students are engaged in GREAT instruction. If students are provided instructional activities that are: Guided by the curriculum, Rigorous with research-based strategies, Engaging and exciting, Assessed continuously to guide instruction, and Tailored through flexible groups, then most students will not have the time or energy to exhibit negative behaviors. The lessons will be fast-paced and engaging.

Students will be challenged with instructional activities that are differentiated to meet their needs. They will work in small, flexible groups with their peers in activities that require sophisticated problem solving. Instead of exhibiting negative behavior to create some excitement or to escape boredom, most students will be engaged with their work.

SETTING THE STAGE FOR RESPONSIBLE BEHAVIOR

Rituals and Routines

All students need solid rituals and routines. They need to have a predictable environment in which there are processes for hanging up their coats, turning in their homework, transitioning to small instructional groups, paying for lunch, and so forth. Teachers and school leaders must ensure that rituals and routines are well established and efficient. They must also be taught and re-taught to students so that they have full knowledge of these expectations.

This predictable environment is especially important for students with disabilities who may have processing or behavioral challenges. By establishing and supporting routines, teachers provide students with a solid structure in which to work. If routines are consistent, students will have fewer opportunities to get distracted or confused or to choose to exhibit irresponsible behavior.

Clear Expectations and Consistent Rewards

All students must also have clear expectations for their behavior. That does not mean that each student must be given a copy of the student conduct manual that explains the expectations and the list of potential consequences for breaking the rules. Students do need that and parents need to sign it, but that is not the focus here.

Students should be well aware of how they are expected to conduct themselves in the classroom and throughout the school. Teachers should share with them that they are expected to respect their peers and the adults in the school. They should come to class prepared to learn, and they should be attentive to instruction and responsible for their actions.

Teachers should not assume that students understand what the expected behavior "looks like" in the school. Teachers should explicitly teach the expected skills and reinforce the students when they demonstrate them. Teachers should provide a positive climate in which clear expectations are in place and students are taught those expectations.

Encouragement and reinforcement should be plentiful. There should be a rich and consistent reinforcement system in the classroom and across the school. This system will be both formal and informal. There should be a set of rewards (e.g., computer time, their choice of activities, etc.) that students can earn as they demonstrate appropriate behaviors. In addition to the formal process, teachers should provide encouraging words liberally. Teachers and school leaders need to be positive and encouraging when students make good choices. They should point out when students are doing well and cheer on their good efforts.

There should also be consistent consequences when students make bad choices. Teachers should be competent in redirecting students who are off task. Their directions should be unemotional and move students toward engagement as quickly as possible. A combination of clear expectations with related instruction in those expectations, liberal encouragement and reinforcement, and efficient redirection will enable the overwhelming majority of students, including students with disabilities, to be successful behaviorally.

FUNCTIONAL BEHAVIORAL ASSESSMENTS AND BEHAVIOR INTERVENTION PLANS

Even when GREAT instruction is provided throughout the school and a strong stage has been set for responsible behavior, some students with disabilities (and some without disabilities) will continue to exhibit negative behaviors. In that case, it will be time to conduct a Functional Behavioral Assessment. This terminology can be quite new, especially to educators who are not certified in special education, but it includes concepts that are often exhibited by outstanding teachers. In fact, you will see the results of a Functional Behavioral Assessment at your nearest church on Sunday morning.

The most difficult area to recruit volunteers in most churches is the preschool program. They have to bend over backward to get volunteers to teach those classes. It can really be a challenge because the teacher only sees the children a couple hours each week and therefore has difficulty getting to know the children, establishing expectations, or providing consistent reinforcement when those expectations are met.

In fact in almost every Sunday morning preschool, there is a three- or four-year-old student who is hardwired to be extremely active. Robert, for example, loves to move around the room and is continuously in motion. He bounces around the class, touches everything, and seems to have an inability to focus on any one task or sit still for longer than a minute. If the church is fortunate, there will be that fantastic teacher who conducts a Functional Behavioral Assessment without even realizing it.

Mrs. Lanier is one of those teachers. Before the Sunday school class starts, Mrs. Lanier walks with Robert to the field just outside of the preschool class. "Robert, I have this new watch and I haven't had a chance to use the stopwatch on it yet. I heard that you are an extremely fast runner. Can you run all the way around the field while I time you to see how fast you go?"

Of course, Robert is more than happy to show off his speed and takes a fast lap around the yard. "Robert, that was incredible. I didn't know you were that fast! I bet you can go even faster. Can you run around the field one more time and try to go even faster?" Robert is more than happy to oblige. After finishing his second lap, Robert is pretty tired and winded. "Robert, that was excellent. Can we go back into the classroom and would you like to have a seat so that we can read that story?"

Without even knowing it, Mrs. Lanier conducts a Functional Behavioral Assessment to determine the function of Robert's high activity. She determines that Robert is hardwired to crave physical activity. He is not happy or content unless he is extremely physically active. After determining the function of the behavior, it is easy for Mrs. Lanier to develop an appropriate Behavior Intervention Plan.

She decides to give Robert an opportunity to use all of his energy and need for physical movement in a constructive activity. By providing an opportunity to meet that need, Robert can then settle down and successfully participate in the Sunday school activities. When he demonstrates appropriate behavior of being on-task, she also provides liberal encouragement regarding his good choices.

When the team of educators comes together to develop a Behavior Intervention Plan for a student with significant behavioral challenges, it is appropriate to discuss what happens before and after negative behaviors occur in order to analyze the function of the behavior (hence the name Functional Behavioral Assessment).

In all, there are two main purposes for misbehaviors: either to get something or to avoid something. The student may be attempting to avoid academic tasks that are too challenging. The student may be attempting to avoid embarrassment in front of his classmates. The student may be avoiding attention from adults or peers.

Students could be seeking a variety of things like attention or approval. In middle schools, it is not uncommon for students to misbehave to earn credibility or acceptance from peers. Jonah, for example, may be consistently argumentative with his teachers. If a teacher says something positive, Jonah dismisses it with something negative. He continually makes comments that interrupt instruction to earn a laugh from his peers.

It would be easy to fall into the pattern of punishing the student for repeatedly showing a lack of respect toward the adults in the room. The more skillful educators would conduct a Functional Behavioral Assessment and determine that the student is merely trying to gain positive attention from his peers. He is looking for reinforcement and acceptance from the girls and boys in the class.

Once the function of the behavior is determined, an effective Behavior Intervention Plan can be developed. Ideally, the interventions on the plan would enable the student to obtain what he is seeking in acceptable ways rather than through misbehavior. It is clear that Jonah is going to get attention from his peers. The educators can either give him an appropriate avenue to get that attention or he is clearly going to do whatever it takes to earn that attention. If educators don't give it to him, then the student will take it.

The effective teacher will make it a point to talk to Jonah in private when the opportunity arises. In fact, it would be ideal if a new teacher could speak to Jonah before the first day of class. Mr. Pines may ask to speak to Jonah when he is seen in the hallway. "Jonah, I heard that you are going to be in my science class and I have heard about you." (Of course, Jonah will assume that his negative reputation has preceded him.)

"I have heard that you are a real leader. Other students seem to look up to you and want to be like you. I'm glad you are going to be in my class. I need a leader like you. Would you mind doing me a favor? I heard that you would be an outstanding leader for a discussion we will be having in our class about our recent weather patterns. If you spend a few extra minutes with me so that we can discuss how to lead this group, would you like to lead this discussion in the class?"

By conducting a Functional Behavioral Assessment and developing a Behavior Intervention Plan that meets the student's function of the behavior, Mr. Pines will give Jonah an opportunity to get what he is seeking — positive attention from his peers. He can gain that attention by showing responsible behavior rather than misbehavior. The student gets his need for attention met and the class has an opportunity to complete meaningful academic activities.

Changing Jonah's behavior will not occur overnight. There are no silver bullets. In addition to providing replacement behaviors, the Behavior Intervention Plan should include the types of reinforcers or encouragement that Jonah will receive when he demonstrates appropriate behavior as well as interventions when Jonah makes bad choices. By approaching negative behavior by conducting a Functional Behavioral Assessment and developing a Behavior Intervention Plan, Jonah will gradually show an increase in appropriate and acceptable behavior.

The Functional Behavioral Assessments and Behavior Intervention Plans described here are fairly straightforward and informal. In actuality, they can range from very simple to a very standardized and complex process. The student's behavior and the difficulty or ease at which the functions of the behavior can be identified will determine the complexity of the Functional Behavioral Assessment and Behavior Intervention Plan.

Many students with disabilities will require a formalized and complex process in which data is collected to determine what happens immediately prior to and following a behavior to isolate what factors are contributing to the student's behavior. By collecting this data, patterns are recognized that particular events occur before or after a behavior that make that behavior reinforcing for the child. Those antecedents that occur before a behavior and those consequences that occur after a behavior can then be modified to decrease the likelihood of the negative behaviors occurring while slowly increasing the frequency of productive behaviors.

The use of Functional Behavioral Assessments is based on the premise that student behavior is a way of communicating what is going on with the student. Through patterns of behavior, students are communicating their needs and their wants. Some teachers are resistant to viewing behavior in this way. Many adults would say, "He should just behave. He should know better."

In part, that may be true. We do want to have high behavioral expectations for students and we want to provide clear limits and consequences for misbehavior. When that misbehavior is evident, however, we have to do more than express our displeasure with the student's actions and expect more. When behavioral patterns exist, we have to analyze those patterns to try and replace those negative patterns with positive replacement behaviors that will allow the student to get those needs met positively.

According to Shawn O'Connor (personal communication, January 31, 1998), all new parents know that their baby's behavior is a way of communicating her or his needs. When an infant begins to cry, Mom and Dad try to determine what she wants. Does her diaper need to be changed? Is she hungry? Does she want to be held? Is she in pain with a diaper rash?

The new parents then approach each of those possible needs. If the baby stops crying when she is picked up, then that may handle it. If she continues to cry, the parent may check the child's diaper, or try to feed her. This trial and error will continue until the baby stops crying, which will signal that her needs have been met.

Unfortunately, as children get older, many teachers and school leaders are resistant to considering behavior as a method of communication. They may be resistant to analyzing those behaviors in a systematic way to try to meet the student's needs. We need to be willing to analyze students' needs and wants based on their behavior as we do for infants.

Questions for Reflection

1. In your school, do you see a relationship between those teachers who consistently provide GREAT instruction and their students' demonstration of positive behavior? Conversely, is there a relationship between teachers who provide ineffective instruction and their students' negative behavior?
2. In your school, are rituals and routines clearly established in each of your classrooms? Are there any teachers in your school who are especially strong at implementing rituals and routines? If so, who are they and what can be learned from them? Are there other teachers who have not implemented rituals and routines effectively? Who are they and what assistance can be provided to them?
3. Across your school, are there clear expectations for students? Does everyone know what they are? Are those expectations taught and demonstrated for students and are they reinforced, encouraged, and rewarded liberally for meeting those expectations?
4. When students fail to meet the behavioral expectations, are teachers and leaders effective at redirecting students and engaging them quickly back to their school work? When consequences are delivered, are they consistent and effective at reducing students' negative behaviors?
5. Are the teachers and leaders in your school effective at conducting informal Functional Behavioral Assessments? Do they continually work to analyze students' patterns of negative behaviors to determine what each student is trying to get or to avoid? Are teachers and leaders then effective at providing replacement behaviors so that students can have their needs and wants met in a positive way?
6. Is there a process in your school to conduct more formal Functional Behavioral Assessments? Are personnel available at your school or through your school district who have the expertise to collect and analyze student observational data to determine the function of misbehavior when less formal Functional Behavioral Assessments have not been effective at improving students' misbehavior?

Chapter Nine

Changing Adult Practices

The first half of this book was devoted to clearly describing the instructional components (GREAT instruction, effective co-teaching, and approaches for improving student behavior) that should be seen in every classroom across the school in order to radically increase the achievement of students with disabilities. The second half of the book is devoted to describing the system of data analyses; professional development; and ongoing coaching, support, and momentum that must be built so that classroom teachers routinely lead and implement those instructional components. In short, the first half was about what needs to happen while the rest of the book describes how to make it happen.

If we are unable to improve the practices of our teachers in the school, then we will see the same results that we have seen previously. The same students who have traditionally been successful will continue to be successful. The students with disabilities who have been less successful will continue to be unsuccessful. The logic is really very simple—if we want to see significant improvements in achievement, then we have to focus our efforts on improving and ensuring teachers' effective practices. Even though the logic is simple, improving adult practices is anything but easy.

That does not mean that all of the responsibility lies on the shoulders of classroom teachers. In fact, the school leadership team that completes this book bears the larger responsibility. They must build extremely efficient systems of support so that teachers have the necessary training and support to improve their practices with fidelity. The school leadership team must improve their own practices so that teachers have the opportunity to make change.

Many initiatives fail in schools because changes never make their way to classrooms. At the end of the day, many, if not most, new instructional initiatives are unsuccessful because many school leadership teams are not effective at changing their own practices and the practices of their teachers.

The next question is obvious. What does it take to change teachers' practices? The answer can be found at your nearest martial arts studio. Let's say that a woman named Elisha is interested in taking martial arts classes. In fact, she has decided to dedicate herself to earning a black belt. She was athletic in high school but became less active as she got older. She not only decides that she wants to earn a black belt, but she also sets a timeline for herself. She sets an ambitious goal of earning that black belt in two years. What does she need to do to improve her "practices" or skillfulness so that she steadily grows as a martial artist, ultimately earning a black belt?

The obvious answer is that Elisha needs practice—lots of it. But she needs other elements also. She needs to find a martial arts studio whose coaches have a history of effectively training adults to become black belts. By finding a studio with that history, she will be sure she participates in an "evidence-based" curriculum, proven effective in assisting the participants in reaching their goals.

It will not serve her purpose to sign up with a martial arts studio that primarily focuses on five- and six-year-old potential martial artists who quickly lose interest in the sport. She needs to be trained by professionals who have established a pattern of assisting athletes in acquiring their black belts.

By enrolling in an established, effective martial arts studio, she can be sure her coach has a clear vision of the end goal. The coach will know specifically what skills Elisha needs to develop to earn a black belt. She has to become adept at performing specific kicks and punches. She needs to complete predetermined sequences of martial arts movements that combine to make a whole. She needs competence in sparring and blocking. Her coach must have a clear and very specific understanding of what Elisha will need to learn and be able to do over the next two years. As Elisha moves through this process, her understanding of those black belt competencies will also become clear and concrete.

In collaboration with her coach, Elisha also needs to determine her starting point. They need to determine her strengths and weaknesses near the onset of her quest. They will determine where she stands on elements like flexibility, strength, and coordination. Based on this analysis, her instructor will undoubtedly try to capitalize on her areas of strength while improving her areas of weakness.

If she is extremely flexible but has poor body strength, she will continue to stretch before every practice and will have a good range of motion in her kicks, but she will spend extra time and energy on improving her body strength. This initial assessment will help determine the specific areas that will assist her in reaching her goals while outlining skill barriers that must be improved as she moves forward.

Elisha also needs an opportunity to practice multiple times each week and to receive systematic feedback from an expert—her coach. She needs to follow the curriculum and receive suggestions, corrections, and encouragement on her efforts. If she is not putting her weight on the correct foot, then her coach needs to point that out. If she is dropping her guarding arm, then she needs to be reminded to focus on that arm. When she hits the bag with power or blocks a punch effectively, Elisha's coach needs to reinforce her correct technique. That systematic coaching will steadily enable Elisha to add and refine new skills on the way to her ultimate goal.

During that process, she will also need to reach benchmarks. Elisha's goal is to attain her black belt in two years. Along the way, she needs to know if she is on pace to meet that goal. The study of martial arts includes a preset system of benchmarking. Potential black belts are tested periodically to see if they can earn the next belt color.

She may go from a white belt to a yellow belt to a green belt and so on until she reaches a black belt. If she does not earn those various rankings in a specific time frame, then she will not be on target to earn her black belt in two years. That progress monitoring will inform her workouts. If she is on target and earns those belts as expected, then she should stay the course. If she loses momentum and fails to keep on pace, then she will need to accelerate her training activities to get back on track.

It is easy to assume that Elisha will learn all of her new skills from her coach. Relying on one person to meet those needs, however, will not be sufficient. Her time frame is very aggressive so she will have to maximize her learning. Therefore, Elisha needs to surround herself with other people who are committed to martial arts. In all likelihood, these folks will be pursuing the same goal at the martial arts studio. Some of her peers will be better than she is and some will be worse. By participating with a cadre of similarly minded individuals, she will learn both formally and informally.

At times, she will receive explicit instruction from her peers. She may ask Thomas to show her how he keeps his balance when he is completing the kicking combination. At other times, she will informally notice that Maria is using her entire body when she punches and that seems to be an effective technique. Elisha will then incorporate those techniques into her own practice. A group of athletes that are working toward the same goal will all benefit from the brainstorming, modeling, motivation, and element of competition that is present in any athletic pursuit.

Elisha also needs one last critical component to reach her goal. She needs to ensure that all of the resources in her life are aligned and focused on achieving this goal. She needs to determine that this is a major personal goal so that there cannot be other competing goals. This is not the time for her to pursue another college degree, for example.

Elisha also needs to recruit people in her life. As a wife and mother of three children, she needs to have some conversations with her husband and children to determine if this is a goal that the family can help her to pursue. Are all of the people in her life aligned to help her achieve her goal? Will her husband and children support her in taking the time it will require to meet her goal?

In summary, it is obvious that in order to change her "practices" as an adult to reach her goal, Elisha will need some very specific components for success. She will need:

- A clearly defined vision of her goal that is shared by her coach and herself. They need to know the specific skills that she will need in order to be considered a black belt.
- A needs assessment that determines her starting point in terms of her physical strengths and weaknesses as related to martial arts.
- Engagement in a proven curriculum.
- Ongoing feedback and coaching from an expert.
- Formative assessments that will provide information so she and her coach can refine her training toward her end goal.
- Participation in a group of peers who are pursuing the same goal in order to formally and informally learn from each other.
- Alignment of the people and resources in her life to ensure that they are all committed to helping her achieve her goal.

The original question was: What does it take to change teachers' practices? It actually takes the same elements to change teachers' practices as it takes to change Elisha's "practices." Teachers need a clearly defined end goal for what instruction should look like in their classrooms. They need to specifically understand the components of GREAT instruction and what they will look like. They also need to receive ongoing coaching and feedback toward that improved instruction.

They need to review their progress against predesigned benchmarks. For teachers, that information will not only determine if their practices are improving over time, but also whether students are showing increased achievement. If students are not learning or if the teachers' practices are not improving sufficiently, then it is clear that the training and support that are provided to the educators must be improved to get both the teachers and students back on track.

Educators need to work with their colleagues, other teachers, and administrators, who are working toward the end goal of improving instruction. They need to benefit from each other's experiences, expertise, brainstorming, and problem solving. They need to be engaged in conversations about the instructional elements they are implementing and the effectiveness for student learning. They need to continually brainstorm with others and observe their colleagues as they work toward refined instructional strategies.

They also need to benefit from aligned resources. All of the personnel in the school, particularly the leaders, instructional coaches, and external supporters, need to be aligned in working toward the same end goal of improved instructional practices. They all must have the same clear vision of what effective instruction should look like in every classroom. Any feedback the teacher receives should be consistent regardless of the specific person who is providing feedback. Coaches, administrators, and other leaders must have carefully defined the critical elements to be observed so they are all looking for the same observable practices. That way, the school will move efficiently toward the same clear end goal.

The job of school leaders, therefore, is to create systems of support, professional development, and leadership (as seen in the martial arts example) that enable teachers to steadily and systematically move their skills toward GREAT instruction. Leaders must build and implement:

- a clear and consistent vision of the expectations for GREAT instruction in every classroom;
- a needs assessment, or data analysis, to determine the starting point for every school year;
- a system of professional development activities that systematically moves teachers toward GREAT instruction;
- mechanisms to provide ongoing feedback and coaching to teachers, utilizing all members of the school leadership team;
- a system of progress monitoring to ensure that teachers are gradually improving their classroom practices and that students' learning is on track to meet the curricular expectations;
- structures so that teachers have the opportunity to formally and informally learn from each other as they work toward implementing GREAT instruction;
- personnel and financial resources that are aligned and focused on GREAT instruction, with minimal distractions and interference.

How does this approach to changing adult practices compare to the "professional development" activities that are usually provided to teachers? Do schools typically provide the type of systematic support, coaching, leadership, and alignment that was described in the martial arts illustration?

Unfortunately, most schools do not operate in this way. Teachers usually participate in a variety of one-shot training activities throughout the school year that are not aligned to one another.

During preplanning days at the beginning of the school year, they may get a brief overview of one instructional strategy. During the initial months of school, teachers will participate in various activities that do not necessarily provide follow-up to the previous training but instead compete with newer initiatives. As the year progresses, even more sporadic professional development experiences are layered upon those initial activities.

In addition, many schools have different expectations placed on teachers by different entities within the school district. The math department from the central office espouses one set of expectations while the special education department has different priorities. The school leaders are responsible for coordinating all of these efforts while themselves adding their own expectations. A clear vision of what is expected has not been established by the members of the leadership team.

Therefore, teachers are responsible for somehow pulling in the variety of expectations and the content of numerous misaligned professional development initiatives and expectations to build a cohesive instructional program. In the end, this scattered approach to improving teachers' practices leads to more ineffective practices or a disregard for all new initiatives.

Our challenge as educational leaders is to overcome these difficulties and align all central office administrators, school-based leaders, internal coaches, teacher leaders, teachers, and external supporters to build aligned systems so that teachers across the school implement improved instructional practices with fidelity. As leaders, we must develop a clear vision of what instruction should look like in every class and provide all of the elements of effective and efficient professional development systems.

The improvements in teachers' practices will ultimately result in the increased achievement of students with disabilities and other students who struggle. While we are building the efficient systems of change, we must also eliminate ineffective practices. We must weed out all of the inefficient activities that are routinely implemented in schools and are barriers to improved instructional practices. We must abandon activities that are not having a positive effect and replace them with activities that are streamlined and efficient and ultimately have a positive impact on teachers' practices and student learning. Over the next few chapters school leaders will learn how to build efficient systems of change while bravely disregarding activities that are clogging their daily calendars and diverting their attention.

Questions for Reflection

1. Describe the professional development activities that have been completed over the past two years in your school. Include all training programs, coaching exercises, and expectations placed on teachers to improve instruction. Are these efforts resulting in significant improvements in teacher practices and student achievement across your school?
2. Over the past two years, have your school efforts to improve adult practices and student achievement reflected the targeted and systematic approach seen in the martial arts scenario or has there been a sense of chaos as competing initiatives and overlapping expectations are rolled out? Explain your answer.
3. If your school does not resemble the martial arts example, what effective components of improving educators' practices were missing and what ineffective activities were conducted?

Chapter Ten

Aligning and Preparing the Leadership Team: Needs Assessment

As a school leader, how do you build ongoing direction and support for your faculty in the same way that the martial arts coach provides for the novice athlete? It would be nice to think that the school principal can act in the exact same role as the martial arts coach and provide the majority of the ongoing coaching and feedback once a good system of professional development has been created. Unfortunately, the responsibilities of the principal are too broad to carry the load alone. In fact, none of the members of the leadership team has sufficient time to lead the charge in isolation.

The principal, assistant principal, instructional coaches, lead teachers, and external coaches all have a docket full of responsibilities. As individuals, they cannot provide the support and leadership that is required to change the practices of all teachers, but in combination they can certainly have the needed impact. The first step to changing teachers' practices across the school is to align every member of the leadership team so that they are prepared to build and implement intensive systems of support, coaching, and leadership.

Initially, the members of the leadership team must conduct a needs assessment to determine the starting point for the school year. This needs assessment must include an analysis of both quantitative and qualitative data over multiple years to help paint a complete picture of the school's strengths, weaknesses, and trends. This analysis should include a review of students' performance based on student achievement data (quantitative data analysis) and a review of teachers' practices as they compare to the components of GREAT instruction (qualitative analysis).

QUANTITATIVE ANALYSIS: STUDENT ACHIEVEMENT

How are the students across the school performing in reading, English/language arts, science, written expression, and mathematics? How are high school students performing in the various high school courses? Over the past few years, has there been consistent progress in every content area or do the data indicate that there are subject areas and/or courses in which the students are underperforming?

In addition to analyzing the performance of the entire student body, the leadership team should analyze the performance of each subgroup. Over multiple years, are there positive trends, negative trends, or is performance relatively flat for each of the subgroups (e.g., different ethnic groups, English language learners, and students from economically disadvantaged homes)? What are the areas of strength and weakness for each of the subgroups? The leadership should also conduct a thorough analysis of the performance of the students with disabilities.

The placement patterns of students with disabilities should also be analyzed. Is your school educating a large percentage of students with disabilities in general education classes? What percentage of students with disabilities in the school spend at least 80 percent of their day in general education classes? What percentage of students with disabilities spend most of their day in pull-out special education classes? How do the data compare to the school district's inclusion rate or the state's inclusion data? Are there more students with disabilities who could be educated in general education classes if GREAT instruction was provided in those classes?

The data analysis should also include a review of other factors such as rates of school attendance. Do students from across the school or students within various subgroups (such as the disability subgroup) have higher than average rates of absenteeism? It is very difficult for students to learn the curriculum, to say the least, if they are not in school. If you determine that absenteeism is a problem, then it is appropriate to dig into the data to determine the cause of the absenteeism.

In some places, school leaders rely too heavily on school suspension as an intervention for inappropriate behavior (especially for students with disabilities who demonstrate behavioral challenges). While suspending students may be appropriate at times, it can also become a default mechanism that does not ultimately improve student behavior. Therefore, the leadership team may determine that absenteeism is having a negative impact on student achievement, but the problem is not primarily due to students and families choosing to miss school. Instead, the problem may be due to ineffective approaches to improve student behavior.

The data analysis will look different for elementary schools, middle schools, and high schools. Typically, achievement data is more available for elementary students. A state test or norm-referenced test may be administered to students in every grade. Therefore, data can be compared across the school for each grade over multiple years. Data can also be analyzed across multiple years for each student to determine if the student is maintaining a certain pace of academic growth.

In middle schools, annual student achievement data will most likely be available as in the elementary schools, but other factors will gain in importance. In some school districts, student misbehavior spikes in middle schools. An analysis of discipline data will reveal what misbehaviors are prevalent across the school. That data can also be used to determine if there are specific times of the day, particular students, or specific locations that are high risk for misbehavior.

You can also dig into data to determine if some students are becoming disenfranchised from school. Multifaceted data analysis that includes class grades, absentee rates, discipline data, and teacher input might reveal middle school students who are high risk for dropping out of school once they reach high school.

In high schools, the data analysis may be more challenging as many high schools do not administer annual assessments of student achievement. In this scenario, a variety of data sources may need to be analyzed. This may include assessments that are given at the end of specific courses in high school, annual assessments from middle school, absentee rates, and so on. High school is also a good time to analyze students' involvement in extracurricular activities. Students who fail to become involved in extracurricular activities may be at high risk for academic failure and dropping out of school.

In high school, the data analysis at the student level will look like a profile. Once that profile is completed for each child, then students can be grouped into three groups: the red group, yellow group, and green group. The green group is moving along well and needs no additional support. The yellow group requires caution and a certain level of support. The red group requires the school leaders and teachers to stop and develop plans for support.

Why should a leadership team devote time to conducting a data analysis? This information will set the foundation for continued actions. As the leadership team reviews the different elements of GREAT instruction, the results of the data analysis will inform their work. If the data indicate that students are underperforming in mathematics but are successful in other content areas, then the leadership team will focus their attention on the components of GREAT instruction as they relate to mathematics. If science is an area of weakness for a particular subgroup, then the leadership team should analyze the elements of GREAT instruction for the specific subgroup in the context of science.

QUALITATIVE ANALYSIS: TEACHER PRACTICES

After considering the performance of students with disabilities, it is time to analyze instructional practices across the school. After each preceding chapter, questions were provided regarding the implementation of each element of GREAT instruction. Now it is time to pull it all together so that your leadership team develops an overall consensus about the instruction that is occurring throughout your school.

Each member of the leadership team should complete the following rating scale independently. They should rate each element of GREAT instruction across their building on a scale of 1 to 10 with "10" indicating that the element is consistently implemented with immense proficiency in every class throughout the school. A "1" indicates that the element is not seen in any class or classroom throughout the school.

You may decide that the members of your leadership team should spend time observing classrooms before they can complete the rating scale or you may have sufficient observational data readily available to complete the scale without further observations. Regardless of the approach that is taken, each member should complete the scale independently first. The members of the leadership team should then openly discuss their individual ratings to develop a consensus on their school's score for each element.

After the members of the leadership team have developed a consensus on the results of this rating scale and completed the quantitative analysis of student performance, priorities will begin to merge.

Your team may determine that the quantitative data reveals that all subgroups of students are struggling in mathematics when compared to English/language arts. A deeper analysis may show that students with disabilities follow that same pattern, but continue to show weaknesses in both math and English/language arts when compared to other groups. The quantitative analysis may reveal that the underperformance in math may be due to a lack of curricular knowledge in mathematics across the board, a lack of varied research-based instructional strategies, and the lack of implementation of small-group instruction based on ongoing data. The patterns of adult practices in these areas are contributing to underachievement in mathematics for all students, but especially for students with disabilities.

Table 10.1. GREAT Instruction Rating Scale

Directions: On a scale of 1 to 10, with "10" being the highest, rate your school on each element of GREAT instruction. This rating should reflect all classes, including general education classes and special education classes.

Elements	Score
Guided by the curriculum	
The instruction that is provided is completely aligned to the curricular standards and the respective pacing charts.	
Teachers have a clear understanding of the student work that will meet the curricular standards in the subjects that they teach.	
Rigorous	
General education teachers and special education teachers maximize every possible minute of instructional time because students with disabilities must learn more than other students in the same time period.	
All teachers have high expectations for students with disabilities by providing instructional activities that enable them to become sophisticated problem solvers.	
Teachers teach toward the proverbial "840" to ensure that the scores for all students "move toward the right."	
Teachers have a deep knowledge of their subject area(s), which they demonstrate in their instruction.	
Research-based strategies (This section may be modified if other research-based instructional strategies have been adopted by the school.)	
In elementary schools, reading teachers effectively analyze students' skills in the five dimensions of reading and explicitly teach those skills based on students' needs (phonemic awareness, phonics, fluency, vocabulary, and reading comprehension).	
Math teachers provide balanced instruction to all students, including students with disabilities, which includes instruction in computation, concept understanding, and problem solving.	
Math teachers provide rich and explicit instruction in fractions, decimals, and percents.	
Teachers routinely provide the modeling, guided practice, and independent practice sequence of explicit instruction ("I do it, we do it, you do it") to students with disabilities regarding content, metacognitive strategies, and activities.	
Teachers routinely implement a rotation of ten to fifteen vocabulary strategies that enable children to connect meanings to words and expand on their knowledge of terms.	
Students with disabilities routinely participate in preteaching vocabulary activities.	
Teachers routinely provide systematic instruction in visual organizers that enables students to go from being provided the visual organizers to ultimately being able to develop a visual organizer from a blank page that effectively reflects major ideas and the relationships between the ideas.	

(continued)

Table 10.1. (*Continued*)

Elements	Score
Research-based strategies	
Teachers routinely provide instruction that enables students to succinctly describe their visual organizers by effectively summarizing and communicating the information.	
Engaging and exciting	
Teachers routinely provide instructional activities that are designed to engage and excite their students.	
All students, including students with disabilities, are routinely actively engaged in their classroom activities.	
Assessed continually to guide instruction	
Across the school, there is an agreed-upon set of formative assessments that are used by all teachers who teach the same grade/subject.	
School leaders and teachers meet regularly to review students' progress on the formative assessments (including class work) and to plan next steps for different groups of students (from high achievers to struggling students).	
It is obvious that teachers alter their instruction based on the results of ongoing formative assessment data to increase learning.	
Tailored through flexible groups	
When observing any classroom (with one teacher or two teachers), it is more common to see small, flexible group instruction than whole-group instruction.	
Teachers build small, flexible groups based on the results of ongoing student data.	
When there are two adults in the room (e.g., co-teaching or a teacher and a paraprofessional), the overwhelming majority of the instruction that is provided involves preferred co-teaching models in which students are separated into groups with each teacher leading a group.	
When coteachers separate the students into small, flexible groups, students with and without disabilities are in the same groups.	
In addition to the elements of GREAT instruction, respond to the statements regarding efforts to promote students' responsible behavior.	
Rituals and routines are well established and most students respond well to those rituals and routines.	
There are clear expectations for student behavior and students are explicitly taught those expectations regularly.	
Encouragement, reinforcement, and rewards are provided liberally to students when they meet behavioral expectations or when they show improvement in their behavior.	
Teachers continuously try to determine the function of students' misbehavior, and they use that information to provide positive options for students to get their needs and wants met.	
There is expertise in the school available if a formal Functional Behavioral Assessment must be conducted in which complex data is collected and analyzed regarding specific students' behavioral patterns.	

Questions for Reflection

1. What did the quantitative analysis of your student performance reveal? What are the strengths and weaknesses for each subgroup of students? Has there been growth over the past few years or has student performance been relatively flat?

2. What does the placement data reveal about your inclusion efforts for students with disabilities? Is your school including students with disabilities at a higher rate that the school district and/or your state? What does the placement data reveal to you about your school?

3. What consensus did the expanded leadership team reach regarding the implementation of GREAT instruction? What are the strong components across the school and what are the priority areas for improvement?

4. What is the relationship between the quantitative student data and the implementation of the various components of GREAT instruction? Is there a connection between weak instructional components and underperformance of students in specific areas or for specific groups of students (e.g., students with disabilities)?

Chapter Eleven

Aligning and Preparing the Leadership Team: Common Expectations

Once the analyses of student performance and adult practices are complete, the leadership team must have a consistent and clear vision of what is expected in every classroom. It is one thing to realize that there is a specific component of GREAT instruction that is weak across the school. It is another to develop a concrete consensus on what should actually be seen in those classrooms.

The martial arts coach must have a clear vision of the competencies of a black belt just as the school leadership team must specifically envision the expectations for GREAT instruction across the school. Earlier in the book, the following question was posed, "If you asked every teacher in your school what constitutes GREAT instruction, how many answers would you get?" In many schools, there would be a different answer provided by every teacher in the building.

Unfortunately, the same is true for every leader in the building. The principal might have a different expectation for GREAT instruction than does the assistant principal or the instructional coach or the department chairs. How can the faculty clearly understand the expectations for their classroom if the definition of GREAT instruction can be so loosely interpreted? How will the teachers move toward GREAT instruction, or even understand it, if each leader in the school espouses different requirements and expectations?

Even worse, many school leadership teams do not define any expectations for classroom instruction. They may require superficial components to be seen, such as the curricular objectives being posted in each classroom, but beyond that they often do not explicitly state what is required and expected instructionally across the school. In that scenario, teachers are left to themselves to implement their version of GREAT instruction, which in many instances is ineffective. Did the martial arts expert allow each new student to identify what skills are needed to earn a black belt? Of course not.

The principal, assistant principal, instructional coaches, teachers from general education and special education, department chairs, and external facilitators (regardless of their specific title in the school) must have a clear, consistent, and specific vision of what GREAT instruction should look like in every classroom in the school (including general education classrooms and special education classrooms). What are the observable components of GREAT instruction that should be evident in every classroom regardless of the grade or the subject that is taught?

Once the leaders have clear and consistent expectations for the school, then they can systematically lead all members of the faculty toward those expectations. In previous chapters, a summary was provided of each element of GREAT instruction. In this chapter, specific, observable actions that the school leaders can expect to see will be described.

GUIDED BY THE CURRICULUM—CLASSROOM INDICATORS

The first step of providing GREAT instruction is ensuring that teachers are providing instruction that is driven by the curriculum. The leadership must determine what indicators will be prioritized to determine if every teacher is teaching according to the curriculum.

As with each element of GREAT instruction, the leadership team must choose a few indicators that yield the highest information about what is occurring in classrooms. What are the one or two concrete, observable indicators that will definitely demonstrate the teacher's instruction is being guided by the standards? One example might be a combination of pacing charts and classroom observations.

Many school districts have developed pacing charts that document when each of the curricula will be addressed and reviewed during the school year. When members of the leadership team are conducting classroom observations, they should be armed with a copy of the pacing chart for the respective grade and subject. That way, the observer can ensure that the instruction that is observed is aligned to the curriculum that should be addressed during that week.

This is not to say that during any particular day, every teacher who teaches a particular subject and grade should be addressing the same standard or completing the same instructional activity. Based on the analysis of ongoing student data, teachers will tinker with their instruction. They may circle back around and review a concept in Tuesday's lesson that was not clearly grasped on Monday. That type of tinkering with instructional plans should be reinforced.

The pacing chart does not dictate lessons on a particular day but highlights what should be covered every week or so. By comparing the pacing chart with the activities seen in the classroom observation, the leadership team will be able to ensure that individual teachers are focusing on the curriculum and are on course to address all of the annual curriculum within the school year.

Reviewing lesson plans is a less reliable way to ensure that teachers are addressing the curriculum. Some teachers develop their lessons and then go back and note the curriculum standards that are being addressed in the lessons. Their planning process is backward. Instead of looking at the curriculum as the student goals and planning instruction from there, the teachers are retrofitting the standards to fit into their existing activities. Unfortunately, just reviewing a teacher's lesson plans makes it difficult to determine if instruction is driven by the curriculum.

In addition to comparing the pacing chart to the instructional activities that are observed, the observer should also see the teacher clearly explaining what students are expected to learn during that instructional period. A third-grade teacher may state, "Students, as you remember we are continuing to work on our multiplication tables that include 9. Today, we are working on our '9s want to be 10s' strategy. Let's read our goal for today from the white board: 'Today, we will practice solving multiples of 9 by using the "9s want to be 10s" strategy.'"

If the observer happened to miss that part of the lesson, he or she can certainly ask the teacher what performance standard(s) he or she is addressing in class. The observer can also ask students what their learning goal is for the day. The students should be able to explain their goal for the day (in developmentally appropriate language).

Since the main goal of this book is to improve the academic achievement of students with disabilities, it is recommended that the observer ask students with disabilities (along with other students) about their learning goal for the day. That way, the observer can ensure that not only is the instruction guided by the curriculum, but that students with disabilities are keeping up with the teacher's instruction. (In keeping with the requirements for confidentiality, students should never be identified in front of others as having a disability.)

Regardless of the indicators that are used to monitor the delivery of instruction based on the standards, the leadership team must determine those indicators that will be the most reliable in reflecting teachers' alignment to the curriculum.

RIGOROUS WITH RESEARCH-BASED STRATEGIES— CLASSROOM INDICATORS

Rigorous

There are many indicators that could be used to ensure that instruction is sufficiently rigorous. The most telling may be to focus on the classroom discussion. Are the teachers asking students questions that require them to use higher-order thinking skills? Are the students' responses sufficiently complex to indicate that they are becoming sophisticated learners? Do the teachers require students to answer questions in complete sentences using the correct terminology (especially in mathematics where informal language and simple answers are often accepted)?

In addition to the discussions that are led by teachers, are the discussions between students demonstrating a thorough understanding of the instructional concepts? Do students routinely ask questions of their peers that go beyond surface-level information? Do students respond with answers that indicate a deeper understanding and an ability to discuss concepts with sophistication?

Once again, it is imperative that the observer notice if students with disabilities are involved in teacher-facilitated conversations that indicate that they are becoming sophisticated learners. It is easy to observe one or two academically proficient students in a class and assume that all students are developing higher-order thinking skills. The observer must ensure that students with disabilities and other students who struggle are becoming sophisticated learners along with the other students in the class.

Research-Based Strategies

In a previous chapter, several research-based strategies were reviewed. The leadership team may choose some of these strategies or use other strategies that are more aligned with the particular needs of the students in their school. As mentioned previously, it is critical that the strategies are implemented with fidelity. Therefore, the leadership team must determine which non-negotiable elements must be seen when those research-based strategies are implemented.

When visual organizers are used within instruction, the leadership team may determine that progress must be seen over time. At the start of the school year, teachers may provide word webs that students use as a structure to add information. Over time, the leadership team should see less guidance as students begin to create visual organizers that are unique for the students, but are used to connect various concepts and illustrate how those concepts are related to one another. By a specified point in the school year, the leadership team should expect to see students beginning with a blank sheet of paper and summarizing information to clearly explain the interrelatedness of the various concepts.

In addition, the school leadership team should expect to see students progressing in their explanations of their visual organizers. At specific points in the year, students should demonstrate the ability to convey the ideas of their visual organizers by explaining the main points and leaving behind the less important details.

As the members of the leadership team conduct classroom observations, they should pay particular attention to how students with disabilities are responding to the use of the instructional strategies, in this case visual organizers. The observer should determine if students with disabilities are grasping the concepts presented and developing and explaining visual organizers to demonstrate a sophisticated understanding of the material.

Regardless of the specific instructional strategy that is being implemented, teachers should regularly be implementing the modeling, guided practice, and independent practice sequence of explicit instruction ("I do it, we do it, you do it"). The leadership team must build a consensus on what explicit instruction should look like. What concrete indicators should be present that indicate that teachers: model the skill, providing guided practice as students implement the skill, and give the students an opportunity to complete the skills independently?

For explicit instruction to be effective, it should occur in context as well as in isolation. Through the years, the educational pendulum has swung between teaching and practicing skills in isolation on one end of the pendulum, to the other end on which all activities are completed within a greater context (e.g., a student-completed project).

The truth is that students need both. They need repeated practice with particular skills in isolation so that they complete enough "turns" to feel comfortable with the skills. Then they need the opportunity to embed those skills into larger contexts.

We can refer back to Elisha and her efforts to earn a black belt in martial arts to demonstrate this point. At times, Elisha will practice an uppercut punch repetitively with both arms. She may do forty repetitions with her left arm and then complete forty with her right arm. That repetitive practice will help make the technique of an uppercut somewhat natural.

She will get to the point where she does not have to think about the specific technique of the punch, like transferring her weight between her feet and using the torque of her upper body to deliver a powerful punch. With repetition, the skill will become automatic.

Elisha also needs the opportunity to place the uppercut in a greater context. She needs to practice her forms, a different series of martial arts moves for each new belt. She will practice the entire series, which includes the uppercut. With this practice, she will learn how to complete a larger context of martial arts moves. At times, she will also spar with her partners and in that context deliver uppercuts in a spontaneous context that includes a little more pressure.

Like Elisha, students in classroom settings need the opportunity to practice skills in isolation and in context. For example, there are several steps to the writing process. To oversimplify, there are prewriting, drafting, editing, and publishing activities. At times, students should be given the opportunity to practice particular steps in that process repetitively without completing the other steps.

To practice the editing phase, students may be given various texts in rough draft and be asked to refine those texts. Those texts can be varied in length from single sentences to multiple paragraphs. After teachers demonstrate editing a short paragraph (and orally speaking their "self-talk" in how they make decisions for editing), they can then provide guided practice to a group of students as they edit a few short paragraphs together. A teacher might ask, "What do you think about this paragraph? Can you think of any ways that we can improve this paragraph?" As students respond, she can help mold and implement their suggestions. Then students can complete several short paragraphs independently with support, as needed, from the teacher. During this repetitive process, students will have enough explicit instruction and practice with the editing skill to acquire proficiency. The editing will become automatic.

At other times, students will combine their discrete skills into the larger context. The teacher might demonstrate how all of the various pieces will fit together into a whole (completing all steps of the writing process in sequence for an assignment). Students will then complete the steps of the entire process with guided support. Finally, students will complete the entire writing process independently with the teacher only stepping in when specific students are getting off track.

The leadership team must develop a consensus on which concrete indicators of explicit instruction should be seen in every class. How will the observer know that the teacher is providing all three elements of explicit instruction—modeling, guided practice, and independent practice ("I do it, we do it, you do it")? Again, the observer should pay special attention to students with disabilities in the room to ensure that they are responding to the instruction with successful skill development.

ENGAGING AND EXCITING—CLASSROOM INDICATORS

The leadership team should also develop a consensus about the level of engagement that should be seen in every classroom. This element is much more difficult to define or describe. You know it when you see it. The leadership team might decide that the best way to determine how effectively teachers are engaging the students is to obviously determine if all students are actively engaged. That seems self-evident. All students in a class should be engrossed in their work. That is not the same as expecting students to be compliant.

At times, an observer might go into a class and see all students sitting appropriately in their seat while the teacher provides a lecture on a science topic. Those students may be obedient and respectful, but they may not be engaged and engrossed in their work. They could be thinking about anything but the topic at hand. In some classes, students don't even try to hide the fact that they are not engaged. You may see students sleeping, passing notes, or being disrespectful. Some students, particularly in some high schools, are so bored that they disengage over time and become high risk for dropping out of school. The expectation is more than teachers merely leading an orderly classroom. Every student in every class should be routinely engrossed in their activities.

As with the other indicators, the observer should pay special attention to students with disabilities. In fact, the observer should closely analyze any student who is not engaged. In a class of twenty-five students, there may be four students who are not actively engaged. Focus on those students. There is a good possibility that at least some of those students have disabilities. At the very least, there is a high probability that they are struggling students regardless of whether or not they have a disability label.

ASSESSED CONTINUOUSLY TO GUIDE INSTRUCTION— CLASSROOM AND OTHER INDICATORS

The leadership team must also determine the indicators that demonstrate if ongoing assessment data are being used to guide continued instruction. These indicators will be somewhat different and more multilayered than the other indicators.

In fact, about half of this work will be done by the school leadership team. The team should be actively involved in analyzing the results of ongoing data and leading the tinkering of instruction based on that data. This will be a paradigm shift in many schools. For many years, school administrators have focused on looking at lesson plans in isolation of student progress. The principal or assistant principal requires teachers to submit their lesson plans for review and approval once a week to ensure that the teachers have planned effectively. According to Baron, the receipt and review of lesson plans should be replaced with the receipt and analysis of formative assessment data. Instead of reviewing the lesson plans, assistant principals and other school leaders should spend their time reviewing the results of formative assessments across the school (K. Baron, personal communication, June 20, 2007).

School leaders should determine if there are trends that need addressing. They should determine if teachers' practices are improving and if students are progressing satisfactorily. If not, how will instruction be adjusted for those students? They should determine which students are exceeding expectations and ensure that instruction is responding to their needs for increased rigor.

The team should pay particularly close attention to the performance of students with disabilities and other students who struggle. By analyzing their data, they will ensure that students who may have traditionally been unsuccessful in school are on track to meet the year-end expectations.

In addition to focusing on the student performance, the analysis of formative data can also assist in determining if there are teachers who are struggling and need additional support to ensure that their students meet or exceed expectations. If large numbers of students in a given teacher's class are failing to meet the standard of competency on formative assessments, then the leadership team should determine the most effective ways to increase support for that teacher.

Therefore, the first layer of indicators for "assessing continuously to guide instruction" is an analysis that the leadership team must conduct of its own performance. Is the team elbow-deep in the ongoing data? Are there standing forms in place that allow for the leadership team to review the data in succinct and informative formats? Are the data routinely generated and prepared in those high-yield ways so that reviewing the data and making recommendations are regularly scheduled activities for the leadership team?

Unfortunately, if you ask many principals about the results of their ongoing data reviews, they might say something like, "My assistant principals complete that activity." As mentioned previously, instructional changes in the school must be driven by the principal and must include all members of the leadership team. Therefore, the first indicator of assessment to guide instruction is that the entire leadership team, including the principal, is actively engaged in analyzing formative data and taking steps to change instructional practices based on the data.

The second indicator will help determine if teachers are adjusting instruction based on that ongoing data analysis. Part of this will be evident outside of the classroom. Once the members of the leadership team have analyzed the data and are equipped with ideas for instructional change, each leadership team member should lead groups of teachers in analyzing the data and making classroom changes concrete. In small groups (with the facilitation of one member of the leadership team), teacher teams will review the results of those assessments and determine how instruction should be altered.

As the leadership team and teacher teams routinely implement this process of using formative assessments, analyzing students' performance, and developing instruction that responds to students' needs, members of the leadership team should be able to ask any teacher at any time about the 20 percent of students, for example, who are having the most difficulty. The teacher should be able to identify the students and to explain how instruction is being adjusted in order to ensure that those students increase their learning.

A member of the school leadership team should be able to say to a teacher, "Which students in your class are exhibiting difficulty as seen on the formative assessments? Please describe the specific instructional strategies that will be implemented for those students over the next three weeks." In addition, the members of the leadership team can ask teachers about the 20 percent of students who are doing very well and how those students will be given additional challenges to ensure that they learn at even higher levels.

By facilitating teacher teams, the members of the leadership team will be able to determine if teachers are becoming more sophisticated in their abilities to analyze the ongoing assessment data and then alter instruction based on those data. The discussions in the teacher team meetings will indicate if teachers are becoming more analytical and responsive to students' ongoing needs.

The last indicator for this instructional component can be seen in classrooms. After participating in the teacher team meetings, the observer can determine if instruction is being differentiated and altered based on the analysis and discussions that have occurred. This is where the most important activity takes place. The analyses, brainstorming, and planning must result in actual classroom changes.

This classroom indicator is inextricably linked to the next component of GREAT instruction, tailoring instruction through flexible groups.

TAILORED THROUGH FLEXIBLE GROUPS— CLASSROOM INDICATORS

The most concrete evidence of utilizing ongoing assessment data to guide instruction is found in the implementation of flexible, small-group instruction.

The leadership team must determine expectations regarding this element of GREAT instruction. There are three factors to consider: (1) the required frequency of small-group instruction, (2) the activities of students when they are not in the teacher-led groups, and (3) the rituals and routines.

The expanded leadership team might determine that small-group instruction should be seen more than 50 percent of the time in any classroom and more often when there are two adults in the room. They may also determine that teachers should be able discuss the rationale for those groups.

The leadership team might also expect all groups of students to be engaged in activities that are meaningful, even the groups that are not being directly taught by the teacher at any particular time. There may be a tendency to provide those students with "busy work" to keep them occupied while the teacher is providing instruction to another group of students. Unfortunately, this approach is counterproductive. Students need to be given meaningful, standards-driven activities when they are not being directly taught by the teacher. At times, these activities will be hands-on and at other times these activities will be paper-and-pencil tasks. But they must always be rigorous and meaningful.

Teachers must also ensure that students have the skills to work successfully in various small-group scenarios. Rituals and routines must be established so that the movement into small groups is smooth and the time in those groups is productive for the students.

On the first day of class, students will not have small-group "skills." Those skills must be taught. Therefore, if an observer notices that attempts to implement small-group instruction result in chaos, he or she can conclude that students need more instruction and support in the rituals and routines for small-group activities.

When conducting observations, the observer should ensure that all students are engaged in meaningful and productive activities toward the curriculum, even when they are not participating in teacher-led activities. In addition, observers should ensure that students have been taught the skills to work in small-group contexts.

CO-TEACHING—CLASSROOM INDICATORS

The expectations for co-teaching classrooms are an extension of the indicators for utilizing small, flexible groups. In co-teaching classes, there are two teachers who can provide instruction to two different groups in the classroom. Therefore, the members of the leadership team must build a consensus that when they observe co-teaching classes, they should see both teachers actively leading separate groups most of the time.

Students may be split into two heterogeneous groups with both groups covering the same curriculum. The activities in the two groups may be different, but the same material is being covered. There may be a large group of students and a small group of students. The small group of students may be receiving targeted assistance such as preteaching or remediation. At times, that group could consist of students who need more challenges. The teacher leading that group is extending the material and providing even more rigorous activities than are provided to the other students. The teachers could also be providing center-based instruction in which the students rotate between the centers. The teachers can lead the instruction at two centers respectively. There can also be one or more independent centers.

With two teachers in the classroom, small-group instruction should be the norm rather than the exception. It should be unusual to see large-group instruction taking place. When it does take place, there should be a reason for it. The observer will know that both teachers are being maximized when they are routinely providing small-group instruction.

The observer should also ensure that the students with disabilities are not routinely placed in segregated groups. They should be embedded in the different groups that are utilized. Students should not be grouped based on any label or demographic information but should be placed based on ongoing academic needs. Care should be taken not to fall into the routine of maintaining the same groups much of the time. Ensuring that groups are based on routine data analysis to target instructional needs, with occasional grouping based on students' interests, should prevent grouping solely based on overall ability level.

Co-teaching environments are an ideal scenario for many students with disabilities. With the almost-constant utilization of small, flexible groups, students will receive a great opportunity for repeated practice, continual feedback, and differentiated instruction. The leadership team must develop the common vision that when co-teaching classes are observed, student instruction in small, flexible groups should be ever-present.

OBSERVATION/COACHING TOOL

As the leadership develops a unified perspective on each element of GREAT instruction and the implementation of co-teaching classrooms, an observation/coaching tool should be developed. An example of an instrument is provided below. The leadership team can modify this tool in accordance with their consensus on the indicators of each element of GREAT instruction. Throughout the observation form, "adult" is used rather than "teacher," indicating that all adults in the classroom should be actively teaching.

Teachers Observed: _____ Other Adults in the Room (i.e. paraprofessional): _____

Observer: _____ Time: _____ to _____ Date: _____

Subject: _____ Number of Students in the Class: _____

Table 11.1. Observation/Coaching Tool

Directions: Place a check in the appropriate box.

GREAT Instruction Is:	1 (low)	2	3	4	5 (high)
Guided by the Curriculum					
The instructional activities observed in the classroom reflect the performance standards that should be addressed according to the district-adopted pacing chart.					
When asked, the students clearly explain what standards are being pursued (in age-appropriate language).	1	2	3	4	5
Students with disabilities are able to explain the standards that are being pursued (in age-appropriate language).	1	2	3	4	5
Rigorous with Research-Based Strategies					
Rigorous					
The adults ask students questions that require sophisticated responses and higher-order thinking skills.	1	2	3	4	5
Students are able to answer questions with sophisticated, multifaceted answers.	1	2	3	4	5
The students ask each other questions that require sophisticated responses.	1	2	3	4	5
Students with disabilities are able to answer complex questions.	1	2	3	4	5

Research-Based Strategies

Maximizing instructional time: Work is waiting for students when they enter the room that requires higher-order thinking skills and connects what the students know to what they will learn.	1	2	3	4	5
The adults debrief students' opening work and transitions to the purpose of the lesson, clearly explaining what standard will be addressed in the lesson today.	1	2	3	4	5
Explicit Instruction—("I do it, we do it, you do it).					
The adults model the skill(s).	1	2	3	4	5
The adults provide supported practice as the teacher and the students complete the skill(s) together.	1	2	3	4	5
The adults allow the students to complete the skill(s) independently.	1	2	3	4	5
Students with disabilities are gaining competence in the skill(s) as the teacher moves through the steps of explicit instruction.	1	2	3	4	5
Engaging and Exciting					
The students are fully and actively engaged with their work.	None	2	½ of students	4	Every student
The activities are designed so that they are engaging for the students.	1	2	3	4	5
Assessed Continuously to Guide Instruction					
There is evidence that the teacher is using ongoing data to determine how to differentiate instruction.	1	2	3	4	5
Tailored through Flexible Groups					
Every adult in the room is actively teaching.	1	2	3	4	5
If there are multiple adults in the room, then the students are split into small groups and each adult is leading a group.	1	2	3	4	5
The instruction in the various groups is differentiated based on the needs of the students.	1	2	3	4	5
The students who are completing independent work are completing meaningful, rigorous activities.					
It is obvious that students have been explicitly taught the rituals and routines for being a part of small, flexible groups in the classroom.					

(continued)

Table 11.1. *(Continued)*

Promoting Responsible Behavior

	1	2	3	4	5
Rituals and routines are clearly established.	1	2	3	4	5
Through their actions, students demonstrate that they understand and implement the rituals and routines.					
The adults provide encouragement to students frequently for demonstrating effort and responsible behavior.	1	2	3	4	5
The adults use targeted redirection effectively when students get off task.	1	2	3	4	5

Comments from the Observer

Directions for the Classroom Adults: After reviewing the information above, write how you will improve one or two items during upcoming lessons.

In this observation tool, explicit instruction is included as the foundational research-based instructional strategy. As the school year progresses, additional strategies may be added, including the use of visual organizers as discussed previously, or vocabulary instruction.

The main point is that every member of the leadership team has a unified vision of each element represented on the observation/coaching tool. Every individual will be needed to conduct observations and provide support to various teachers in the school.

By creating a common and concrete understanding of each element of GREAT instruction, your team will ensure that every teacher in the school will receive the same message continuously. Regardless of who conducts the observation (e.g., the principal, assistant principal, department chair, instructional coach), the teacher will hear the same message.

It should be noted that an observer will rarely see every element that is documented on the observation form. Unless an observer spends an entire period in the classroom, for example, it may not be possible to determine if work was waiting for students when they entered the classroom. In that instance, the observer should leave that indicator blank.

It should also be noted that this coaching/observation tool only includes the most telling indicators. It does not include elements that are less reliable indicators of the quality of the instruction in the room.

Many observation tools include an indicator that the performance standard is posted in the room or that there is an instructional bulletin board in the classroom. It is certainly ideal that these elements are in place, but they are not reliable indicators of the effectiveness of instruction. A teacher can post the performance standard daily, but that does not necessarily mean that the students are pursuing the standard or that instruction is effective. The bulletin boards in the classroom can be engaging and instructional, but again, that does not necessarily reflect the instruction that is occurring.

As school leaders, we must focus on instruction. If less reliable indicators are prioritized, some teachers will focus on fixing the bulletin boards or posting the performance standard rather than digging a little deeper and changing their instructional patterns.

This coaching/observational tool also includes an opportunity for teachers to reflect on their practices and respond in writing how improvements will be made. Ideally, the observer and the teacher will have an opportunity to discuss the observation and brainstorm what was effective and what needs adjusting. After that discussion, the teacher can submit written comments on the form. At the end of the day, the ultimate goal is to improve teachers' practices so that GREAT instruction is seen routinely in every class in the school. This instrument is developed and used as a coaching tool toward that end.

Questions for Reflection

1. What specific indicators will you expect to see in classrooms that indicate that instruction is aligned to the curricular expectations? Your answers should go beyond the expectation that teachers should post the curriculum standards that are being addressed.
2. What specific teacher practices and student activities will you expect to see in classrooms to indicate that instruction is sufficiently rigorous?
3. Describe three to four specific research-based instructional strategies that will be implemented across your school. Describe the specific components that should be seen when these instructional strategies are utilized. What specific expectations do you have for the implementation of those instructional strategies?
4. When conducting classroom observations, what will the members of the leadership team look for to determine if students are sufficiently engaged and excited by their class activities?
5. Describe the formative assessments that will be implemented across grade levels/subject areas to gauge student's progress toward the curricular expectations. Will the school utilize Curriculum Based Measures, for example, and/or will teachers develop common assessments?
6. As the leadership team, what expectations do you have for teachers to utilize flexible groups as a component of their daily instruction? How often do you expect to see small-group instruction in teachers' classrooms and how will you determine if the flexible grouping patterns are established based on ongoing formative assessments?
7. Describe the expectations that you will have for co-teaching teams in your building (regardless of the adults' particular job title). What expectations will you have for each shared team to utilize flexible group instruction to differentiate for students' individual needs?
8. As a leadership team, develop an observational tool (or modify the tool in this book) that reflects your common expectations for each element of GREAT instruction.

Chapter Twelve

Align All Programs and Initiatives toward GREAT Instruction

Once the leadership team has a consistent understanding of each element of GREAT instruction, the next step toward ultimately improving teacher practices is to align all of the initiatives and programs in the school toward GREAT instruction.

Schools are responsible for providing varied programs and services for different students. There are special education programs for students with disabilities, Title I programs for students who are designated as economically disadvantaged, and Title III programs for students who are English language learners, for example. In addition to those Title programs and others, schools implement new textbook series almost annually for different subjects.

There are different initiatives that come from the school district or the state department of education. There are new curriculum standards, new schoolwide behavioral approaches, and new instructional expectations. Many of these activities are supported with different funding sources so that implementation and bookkeeping for specific efforts can become isolated from the rest of the school.

The problem with the multiple initiatives is the negative impact that they have on teachers. Because of the various expectations and requirements for the different activities, it is easy for classroom teachers, and the school leaders for that matter, to feel that all of their efforts are disconnected and ultimately at cross-purposes. The various record-keeping activities that teachers are asked to complete and the varied instructional activities seem in competition with one another. Classroom practices suffer from a lack of clear focus.

To successfully change teachers' practices so that they are able to implement GREAT instruction, the leadership team must make sense of all of the swirling activities and expectations. This process is easier than one might expect. At the core of each of these initiatives and programs is instruction. Ultimately, they are all about or can be shaped to support the vision of GREAT instruction. The Title programs, for example, are moved forward with GREAT instruction. All subgroups of students, including those with disabilities, those from economically disadvantaged circumstances, and those students who are English language learners, to name a few, will benefit from each element of GREAT instruction.

The same can be said for new textbook adoptions or new instructional initiatives promoted by the school district or the state department of education. They can all be centered on implementing GREAT instruction. The problem is that leadership teams do not see the commonalities between the various expectations. Therefore, teachers cannot see that their efforts can be streamlined and aligned.

It is imperative that the leadership team align all of the initiatives and communicate them to their staff so that they see them as different elements of the same purpose. The various activities must be hung on the existing structure of GREAT instruction.

If the school district adopts a new textbook series in math, then the leadership team demonstrates to the math teachers how the series includes formative assessments that are a component of GREAT instruction, aligns in part to the state-directed curriculum, allows for the use of research-based strategies, and fosters the efforts to provide rigorous instruction to the students. The leadership team should clearly explain that the new textbook series is one tool that will help them implement GREAT instruction. It is not something else that competes with existing efforts.

The same can be said for the paperwork and activities that are required for special education services. As mentioned previously, an Individual Education Program (IEP) must be developed for every child who has a disability and participates in special education and related services. It includes a description of the impact that the disability has on the student's educational efforts, specific goals that will be addressed at school, and the special education and related services that will be provided to the student.

The IEP can easily become a voluminous document. The leadership team must demonstrate how the process of developing the IEP contributes toward providing GREAT instruction. The IEP goals for each student, for example, should assist the student in achieving the curricular expectations. In many cases, the assessments noted on the IEP should be the same as the formative assessments that are used to guide continued instruction, a vital component of GREAT instruction.

According to O'Connor and Williams (2006), an IEP, once developed, should enable a child to meet or exceed expectations on the statewide assessments. If a student's IEP does not sufficiently describe actions that will enable the student to meet or exceed expectations, then the IEP should be reworked.

This type of alignment and continuity can be established for almost all activities, programs, and initiatives that enter a school. It is the job of the leadership team to reshape and connect each of those efforts for the faculty so that they support the momentum to provide GREAT instruction rather than being an unrelated effort.

It takes a tremendous amount of insight and determination to clearly align and communicate this type of streamlining for your staff. Unfortunately, many leaders are not able to align their initiatives within their building, and they are somewhat overwhelmed by the various competing expectations. These expectations are not likely to go away, but the effective principal must be willing to make sense of all of the various initiatives and programs for the faculty and staff.

In an effort to align the various initiatives and programs, school leadership teams must be willing to reshape information that is shared with the school staff. As the various expectations are shared with the Title providers, the special education staff, and the teachers of students who are English language learners, for example, school leaders should help link the initiatives so that all members of the faculty and staff see how they are connected and directed toward improving instruction.

This does not mean that leaders should try to filter information. In this day and age of complete information access, trying to filter information would be seen as manipulative and would create distrust in the school building. Instead, school leaders should reshape information so that the faculty and staff can envision how the various initiatives are related. Leaders should stress the commonalities about instruction rather than the processes that differentiate the initiatives and programs.

Central office personnel also have a role in the alignment of the various programs and initiatives. Because of the mere size of the various Title programs, for example, different departments within the central office may manage the implementation of Title I and Title III. With the various departments, it is easy for the multitude of initiatives to seem extremely unrelated to one another once they make their way to the schools. Central office personnel should make a concerted effort to align and streamline their efforts and activities so that they arrive at schools seemingly more connected.

Questions for Reflection

As the leadership team, how will you align all initiatives and programs within the school so that they converge in a unified effort to providing GREAT instruction? How will you center all activities (e.g., special education programs, Title programs, foreign language activities, math instruction, and services for English language learners) on the concepts of GREAT instruction? How will you unite all professionals in the building, regardless of their specific job title or activities, so that they are all united around providing GREAT instruction?

Chapter Thirteen

Equipping Teachers to Provide GREAT Instruction

The first step toward implementing GREAT instruction in every class across the school was to align all of the school's leaders so that they have a common and clear vision of GREAT instruction. The second step was to align all of the various school initiatives and programs toward systematically improving instruction. Those two components prepare and equip the leadership team to lead the troops effectively. This type of alignment and unity among all of the school leaders establishes an extremely strong foundation for the next phase of activities, which involves systematically changing the practices of every teacher in the school.

It would be ineffective to gather all of the school's teachers in a faculty meeting and declare that the school will now be implementing GREAT instruction in every classroom. Merely announcing new expectations, no matter how clever or engaging the professional development activity, is not sufficient to improve teachers' practices in a systematic and reliable manner. As mentioned in an earlier chapter, learning new skills takes time, effort, and practice. Teachers need the opportunity to try out new skills and work together to refine those skills until they are able to implement better practices with fidelity and effectiveness.

The purpose of this chapter is to describe a process for systematically moving toward more effective practices. Instead of merely announcing and then expecting improved practices, a specific sequence of activities will be described that, if implemented, will provide a supportive structure so that all teachers can gradually and effectively move toward GREAT instruction.

You may have noticed over the last few chapters that our discussion has focused on changing the practices of all teachers throughout the school in order to improve the achievement of students with disabilities. As we mentioned earlier, students with disabilities are educated in practically every classroom across a school. They are educated in general education classes where there is only one teacher, general education classes where there are coteachers, and special education classes. Our efforts to improve the performance of students with disabilities, therefore, will only be successful if we impact the instruction provided by all teachers.

There is extremely good news here. Our efforts to improve the practices of all teachers toward GREAT instruction will impact the performance of all students—high achievers, average students, those who struggle but do not have a disability label, and students with disabilities. Therefore, the time committed to improving the practice of all teachers for the benefit of the disability subgroup, will have a big pay off as all students demonstrate higher achievement.

IMPLEMENT FORMATIVE ASSESSMENTS

In the previous chapter, a description was provided of the specific decisions that the leadership team should make as they specify each component of GREAT instruction. In order to maximize efficiency, the team should implement those decisions in a very specific sequence. The first activity should be to implement the formative assessments that were decided upon by the members of the leadership team (that includes teacher leaders).

During the first few weeks of school, the formative assessments should be established for all courses for the entire school year. The only exception may be in a school in which the teachers teach all content areas. This situation may be seen in kindergarten through third grade where the teachers teach all subjects. In that situation, it may be overwhelming to introduce all formative assessments during the first weeks of school during the same school year. One or two of the subject areas can be delayed until midway during the school year so that the teachers are not overwhelmed.

There is power in teacher teams developing their own common formative assessments. Whether or not teachers develop them, in order to implement the formative assessments, teachers must have a copy of them and must be trained on their administration. The members of the school leadership team should discuss when each of the formative assessments will be given and how the results of the assessments will be used to guide instruction.

Minimally, the formative assessments should be administered at least every three weeks and the results analyzed as quickly as possible after administration. The goal with formative assessments is to get the biggest bang for the buck. Ideally, the formative assessments will require minimal time for the teacher and students while providing optimal information.

Once teachers are equipped with the formative assessments, many teachers will naturally shape their instruction so that the curricular standards are being addressed in the classroom. So even before the first formative assessments are administered, they will have an impact on classroom instruction.

UTILIZING TEACHER TEAMS TO ANALYZE FORMATIVE ASSESSMENT RESULTS

As the formative assessments are being established, the leadership team should develop a process and a schedule for teams of teachers to meet to review the results of the formative assessments and brainstorm how those results should impact ongoing instruction. These meetings should occur after each administration of the formative assessments. They should be scheduled accordingly and identified as a top priority for the teachers. At least one member of the leadership team should facilitate each teacher group.

Traditionally, it has been common for teachers to have planned meetings to discuss student progress. Seldom do those meetings ultimately result in increased student achievement. First and foremost, the meetings must center around the discussion of the students' performance on the formative assessments. They should be structured so that teachers review students' progress on the assessment and use that information to shape continued instruction.

The teachers should discuss which students are easily meeting the expectations on the formative assessments, and describe specifically how those students are performing in their classrooms. How are they demonstrating a deep understanding of the material? What explains the students' success? What should be done in upcoming instruction to continue to challenge them to meet high standards?

Next, the teachers should discuss the specific students who are not meeting expectations on the assessments. Are there common threads across the students? Are they evidencing weaknesses in the same area? What kinds of errors or weaknesses have been observed in their work? How should instruction be altered to ensure that students' needs are met?

At subsequent formative assessment meetings, teachers should expand their discussions by reviewing how students responded to the strategies that were discussed at the previous meeting and then implemented in the classroom. The flow of these discussions may proceed in this manner:

Each teacher reports on the students who achieved at higher levels as seen on the previous formative assessment. They should then briefly explain the strategies that were recommended at the previous meeting and the students' performance on the most recent formative assessment.

Each teacher then reports on the students who did not meet expectations on the previous formative assessments. The teachers will briefly review the strategies that were recommended and report whether the students met expectations on the following formative assessment.

Each teacher finally reports on any student who is new to either category: those students who exceeded or did not meet expectations on the most recent formative assessment. Instructional strategies will then be brainstormed.

By following this process, students who are exceeding, meeting, or failing to meet expectations will be discussed regularly and systematically. By implementing these structures for formative assessment reviews and ensuring that teachers make these meetings a priority, the leadership team will enable teachers to benefit from each other's expertise while successfully responding to student needs.

EXPANDING THE CONVERSATION—FLEXIBLE GROUPS

Once the teachers become accustomed to the routine of administering formative assessments and meeting in teacher groups (with ongoing direction from a member of the leadership team) to brainstorm instructional interventions systematically, it is time to expand the discussion to include flexible grouping. At this point, the teacher groups should begin to discuss how flexible grouping can be utilized to respond to the results of the formative assessments.

This discussion should develop smoothly and naturally from the existing conversations. In fact, many teachers will automatically discuss flexible grouping patterns that should be implemented when they brainstorm instructional interventions. However, some teacher teams will need to be prompted to include this approach in their discussions and practices.

Depending on the specific data and the instructional strategies utilized, a teacher may implement either homogeneous or heterogeneous groups. A group of students who need specific instruction in a weak area may be brought together to work on those particular skills for a few days. Or the groups could be heterogeneous and include students with a variety of skill levels. The groups should not be static, a practice that could unintentionally establish negative tracking patterns for the students. By extending the formative assessment teacher groups to include the discussion of flexible grouping patterns, your school's teachers will add another element of GREAT instruction.

The discussions of flexible groups will be further enriched for coteachers. They will not only discuss the results of the formative assessments and potential grouping patterns, but they will also discuss how each of them will work together to provide instruction to the flexible groups. They will assign themselves to particular groups that are approaching particular standards. They will discuss how the groups will be managed and the details that will make implementation run more smoothly and effectively.

PROFESSIONAL DEVELOPMENT CONTINUED WITH EXPLICIT TRAINING

The teacher discussions described above can be an extremely beneficial facet of professional development. By focusing on the connection between continually refining instruction and its impact on student achievement, teachers will invariably improve their instructional practices.

This facet of professional development should be combined with explicit training in specific instructional strategies, monitoring, and peer observations. Members of the leadership team can provide this training since they have previously determined the individual components of specific research-based instructional strategies that should be seen across the school. The training could also be provided by teachers in the school who are extremely competent in the instructional strategy. They may be ongoing members of the leadership team or be enlisted because of their facility in their classrooms.

The training may occur during weeks in which the teachers do not meet to discuss formative assessments. For the first eight weeks of school, training activities may be provided every other week on utilizing visual organizers and implementing effective vocabulary/language instruction. By focusing on the specific instructional strategy and providing trainers with multiple opportunities to provide information and teachers with a forum to share their experiences and ask questions, all of the teachers in the school will steadily improve their skills. In eight weeks or so, teachers will be implementing visual organizers as described earlier in the book.

During the first and second training sessions, various visual organizers may be introduced that match specific subject matter content. One type of visual organizer could be discussed as an effective way for students to organize information that includes historical facts. A different type of visual organizer may be presented as an effective way for students to organize two sides of a political argument. By the end of the eight-week period, the trainer will share the ultimate expectations for the use of the instructional strategy for both teachers and their students.

The teachers will understand that they should steadily enable students to perform at deeper levels. The teachers should also minimize their prompts so that students can eventually develop visual organizers from blank sheets of paper. The students should also become competent in succinctly explaining their visual organizer, either verbally or in writing, so that their teachers and peers understand the complex relationships between the various components on the visual organizer.

The same process can be established for implementing effective vocabulary/language instruction. Therefore, the same training sessions (or subsequent training sessions) can be the context for providing explicit training and discussion on vocabulary instruction.

Even though a trainer may be leading these sessions, there should be a significant amount of time available for the teachers to work in small groups and discuss the implementation of the instructional strategies. These training sessions will probably not last more than one hour and ideally would occur during teachers' planning periods. In that way, the trainer's schedule includes leading small-group sessions all day during the same day. For some schools, the sessions may be even shorter, as some elementary schools, for example, may be limited to a thirty-five-minute planning period.

Teachers' planning time, however, is not the only time when this training can occur. Some schools have a segment of time after the students leave and before the teachers' workday ends. That time may be utilized as long as the trainer is extremely engaging. He or she will have to be entertaining and dynamic to compete with the teachers' fatigue and distraction at the end of a long day.

As the teachers become more proficient in the specific instructional strategy, the leadership team will introduce another instructional strategy. In the martial arts example, Elisha steadily became more proficient, in part, because her coach systematically introduced new skills that became building blocks for more skills. This same approach should be taken by the school leaders. As teachers demonstrate proficiency in implementing a few instructional strategies with fidelity, other research-based strategies should be introduced in the training sessions and then reinforced in subsequent discussion groups.

MONITORING AND COACHING

The leaders must also provide follow-up support and monitoring in classrooms to ensure that all elements of GREAT instruction, including the research-based strategies, alignment with the curriculum, and the utilization of flexible groups, are being implemented effectively. Previously, your leadership team developed a common understanding of each element of GREAT instruction. Then you either developed your own coaching/observation tool or modified the tool provided in this book.

The leadership team should use the tool to compare teachers' practices with the criteria for implementing each element of GREAT instruction. At some point following the observation, the individual from the leadership team who observed the teacher should provide feedback in a constructive and positive manner. This type of observation is not necessarily intended to be the official observation for personnel evaluations, but should be similar to what is seen in that martial arts studio—an opportunity for a professional to provide feedback to a colleague.

In order for observational coaching to be effective, feedback needs to be provided on a regular basis. The problem is that school principals are inundated with responsibilities. It would be nice if they had a couple of hours every day to spend in classrooms making observations and providing constructive feedback to teachers. That is not the case. The same can be said for all members of the leadership team: assistant principals, instructional coaches, lead teachers for special education, department chairs, other teacher leaders, and external support personnel.

However, each of those professionals does have some time to spend observing classrooms and providing consistent feedback. The leadership team should collaborate to develop a schedule in which each leader spends time observing teachers in classrooms and providing feedback. By combining efforts, they can devote a significant amount of time to providing the needed support.

This is where aligning the leadership team really pays off. If all members of the leadership team have a strong understanding and a clear consensus of the important characteristics of every element of GREAT instruction, then they will provide consistent feedback to all of the teachers in the building. Once teachers begin to hear the same type of expectations from every school leader, then momentum will build and teachers will move toward improving instruction with fidelity.

This alignment and persistent presence will also circumvent one of the barriers to school improvement that is seen in many schools. When they see all leaders are on board, teachers will be less likely to take the position that this new initiative is a passing fad that will quickly fade. Teachers will see that there are streamlined and focused expectations combined with the needed support, which will be in place for the long term.

SUPPORT HIGH-NEED TEACHERS

In every school, there are teachers who need more intensive support. These high-need teachers may need additional mentoring and coaching because they are new to the field or because they are showing systemic weaknesses in instruction or classroom management.

The leadership team must ensure that the high-need teachers get additional support beyond the teacher team meetings, explicit training, and coaching/ monitoring that is provided to every teacher. Just as the martial arts coach will provide more intensive feedback to the struggling martial artist who is trying very hard, the leadership team must provide more intensive support to high-need teachers.

Each of these teachers must be assigned a partner from the expanded leadership team. The partner must provide more frequent monitoring/coaching activities than he or she does for teachers who are more comfortable with their classroom skills. High-need teachers may need to receive two monitoring/coaching visits a week from that individual. The member of the leadership team should use the coaching/observation instrument and then meet with the teacher after each observation.

The high-need teacher will need the indicators explained so that the teacher is comfortable with the next steps for instructional improvement. Then, later in the week, the leadership team member should conduct another observation in order to view the specific elements that were discussed in the previous meeting. Each observational session should be followed by brainstorming and direct discussions about what is expected during the next observation.

When the expanded leadership team meets, specific discussions should occur about the growth of the high-need teachers. Again, some of these high-need teachers will be considered so merely because they are new teachers. Even if they are extremely effective teachers, they need the nurturing and systematic support that any person needs as they enter a new profession. This will ensure that new teachers develop effective practices from the beginning rather that resorting to ineffective practices.

Other teachers are considered high-need teachers because they demonstrate weaknesses. The leadership team should regularly discuss the progress that all of the high-need teachers are making toward GREAT instruction. The discussions should be very specific regarding the suggestions that were made and each teacher's attempt at incorporating better practices into their daily classroom delivery.

These discussions can become very sensitive. If it becomes obvious that some high-need teachers are not making progress, then the expanded leadership team should most likely no longer discuss them. These individuals become personnel issues. They have a certain right to confidentiality. The principal and his or her designees should discuss in private conversations high-need teachers who fail to make adequate progress.

The high-need teachers who fail to make adequate progress will fall into one of two categories. At this point, your expanded leadership team has provided a significant amount of training and support. You have provided an opportunity for teachers to discuss the results of formative assessments in teacher teams (led by a member of the leadership team). You have provided ongoing explicit training and you have provided intensive and specific support through twice-a-week observation/coaching sessions. These teachers can be categorized as: (1) not having the capacity to show improvement, or (2) not willing to show improvement. Regardless of the category, it is time for next steps. Both groups of teachers should be placed on a formal improvement plan if that process has not already occurred.

The first group of teachers, those who do not have the capacity for improvement, will need to find other employment. This, of course, gets tricky as various rules govern this process in different states and school districts.

Regardless of the process, the school principal now has an enormous amount of documentation on the opportunities that have been provided to teachers in this group. You have provided training, small-group discussions in teacher teams, and twice-weekly observation/coaching sessions. The coaching/observation tool demonstrates the recommendations that were provided, the teacher's written response to those recommendations, and documentation of follow-up observations. You also have sign-in sheets for training and the small-group teacher teams.

The other group of teachers has the capacity to show improvement but has not shown the willingness to implement improved practices. An extremely direct discussion needs to occur with these teachers in coordination with the development or revision of their formal improvement plan. They need to be provided with a clear set of expectations for improvement and potential consequences if those improvements are not observed.

They are obviously demonstrating extreme resistance to improving their practices. This cannot be tolerated. If we are going to improve the achievement of all students, and students with disabilities specifically, teachers cannot show unwillingness to improve their craft. At the end of the day, the principal may need to usher those individuals into another line of work as has been done for those teachers who do not have the capacity for improvement.

PROMOTE PEER OBSERVATIONS

In addition to the observations conducted by the school leaders, teachers should be given the opportunity to spend time making peer observations. However, the purpose of peer observations is quite different than the observations provided by members of the leadership team. According to Showers and Joyce (1996), the purpose of peer observation is not to provide feedback to the teacher or to evaluate the effectiveness of the classroom practices, but to learn from other teachers. In fact, teachers should be discouraged from providing feedback. The observer, rather than the one who is observed, will benefit from the opportunity to see others implement their craft.

Guiding questions or other tools based on GREAT instruction can give observers a framework for the observations. These type of observations coupled with the work of the teacher teams and the ongoing training can have a positive impact on teachers implementing new skills with fidelity and effectiveness.

SUMMARY—CHANGING TEACHER PRACTICES

The real challenge to radically improving student achievement is to build systems to steadily and systematically improve teacher practices with fidelity. Teachers need a structured system for improving their practices toward a well-defined end goal. The leadership team members will develop a consensus on specifically what each element of GREAT instruction should look like in their school. By creating that consensus, the leadership team will develop clear expectations for their faculty.

The next step, as discussed in the previous chapter, is to align all of the programs and initiatives in the school. All initiatives in the school focus on improving instruction, but it is easy to get lost in the details of each initiative and program and lose the focus on effective instruction. The leadership team should align each of those initiatives and programs so that teachers are able to see them as components of the same process to get to the same end—improving student achievement through GREAT instruction.

Once the school personnel and initiative alignments are in place, school leaders should implement specific, concrete steps to improve the practices of their teachers over time. They should facilitate the selection or development of common formative assessments that can be used across teachers who teach the same subject, grade, or course. The formative assessments should be aligned to the curricular expectations and should provide teachers with valuable information that can inform their continued instruction.

Once the formative assessments are in place, the leadership team should schedule small-group teacher meetings in which the teachers share the results of the most recent formative assessments and discuss how that information informs continued instruction. These discussions should include the establishment of flexible groups to meet students' needs. These teacher groups should also discuss the instructional strategies that will be steadily and systematically implemented across the school. In addition, coteachers will brainstorm how they will maximize their impact by implementing small, flexible group instruction based on the results of the ongoing data.

In addition, explicit training activities should be provided by members of the leadership team to provide the faculty an opportunity to discuss the implementation of each element of GREAT instruction. The members of the leadership team will also collaborate to provide classroom observations with constructive and positive feedback to the teachers. Even though each leadership team member is unable to commit the necessary time to observations, their combined efforts can create a significant presence in classrooms. Finally, teachers need the opportunity to conduct peer observations, not for the purpose of evaluating their peers' practices, but for the purpose of being exposed to different colleagues implementing their craft.

This approach to changing teachers' practices may seem overwhelming, but over time it will seem natural and completely related to the instruction that takes place in classrooms. Traditionally, schools have provided minimal support and intensity to improve the practices of teachers. Consequently, many instructional initiatives fall short of truly changing adult practices and student achievement. By implementing all of these complementary steps, teachers will use and refine their practices with fidelity and students will demonstrate improved achievement.

Questions for Reflection

1. In your school, describe the formative assessments that will be used among teachers who teach common subjects, grades, or courses. What is the schedule for the administration of those assessments? (At a minimum, the formative assessments should be administered once every three weeks.)

2. Describe when small groups of teachers will meet to discuss the results of the formative assessments. Make a schedule for their meetings and assign at least one member of the leadership team to be an ongoing member of each teacher group.

3. Develop an agenda for the formative assessment teacher meetings that will ensure that the teams discuss the performance and strategies for students who are exceeding expectations and those students who are not meeting expectations (including students with disabilities in both

groups of students as appropriate). Provide an opportunity at consecutive meetings to discuss the progress that students have made as a result of the instructional interventions that were implemented.

4. Describe the schedule that will be used to provide explicit professional development activities for your teachers. Who will provide the training and which instructional strategies will be taught in what order?

5. Describe how the members of the leadership team will conduct classroom observations. Assign each member of the leadership team to specific teachers for their observations. As the year progresses, match high-need teachers with specific members of the leadership team. How will you gather the data from the observations/coaching sessions that are conducted twice a week?

6. Describe how teachers will be given the opportunity to conduct peer observations.

Chapter Fourteen

Quit Doing Stuff That Doesn't Help

There are three main messages in this book. First, students with disabilities need one critical element in schools in order to meet academic standards. They need GREAT instruction. In fact, GREAT instruction is the "silver bullet." There is nothing else that will enable students with disabilities to meet the academic standards. The second message is that many students with disabilities can successfully access GREAT instruction in general education classes. In many schools, it is appropriate to increase the percentage of students with disabilities who increase their time in general education classes.

Even though GREAT instruction is the "silver bullet," it will take great effort to implement. The third message in this book is that GREAT instruction will only occur routinely and consistently if the members of the school leadership team are effective at changing the practices of their teachers. They must do this by radically changing their own practices so that they build the structure, training, monitoring, and ongoing support that teachers need to change their practices.

Unfortunately, in many schools, there are practices that are undermining the ability to implement GREAT instruction. There are many activities that are routine in schools that not only differ from GREAT instruction, but create a barrier toward moving in the direction of GREAT instruction.

Time is our most important resource. Unfortunately, our limited time is often wasted as we implement ineffective practices, thereby interfering with the ability to move toward GREAT instruction. Therefore, the leadership team in your school must decide to implement the activities in this book while activities that do not contribute toward the main vision will be completely discontinued if at all possible or minimized if they absolutely must continue. A description of various activities that should be eliminated or minimized in your school is provided.

DISCONTINUE INEFFECTIVE PROFESSIONAL
DEVELOPMENT ACTIVITIES

Professional development systems that systematically improve the practices of teachers over time have been described earlier in this book. Effective professional development will include:

- Aligning all leaders in the school.
- Aligning initiatives and programs throughout the school.
- Establishing formative assessment for students.
- Establishing regularly scheduled teacher meetings for teachers to discuss their students' progress on formative assessments and how that information impacts the development of flexible groups.
- Explicit training on each targeted instructional strategy that allows teachers to delve deeply into them over time to develop fidelity of implementation.
- Nonjudgmental peer observations among teachers so they learn from each other.

Changing adult practices will take all of these components. Invariably, you will have people on your leadership team or in the school who will suggest that the school provide a one-shot training activity on a particular strategy or who will ask to attend a conference centered on a particular trend in education. These types of professional development activities do not improve teachers' or leaders' skills with fidelity any more than one lesson by the martial arts coach will improve Elisha's martial arts skills.

Financial and time investments in one-shot workshops, even if they cover multiple, consecutive days, rarely improve teacher practices. Let's pretend that a teacher or a leader actually asked the question with that information intact: "Can I attend a conference on a new instructional strategy that will take me out of the school for three days, that will cost a registration fee of a few hundred dollars, but will not change my practices with fidelity so it will ultimately have no impact on the academic achievement of my students?" Your answer as a school leader would most definitely be no.

Unfortunately, professionals in education have been acculturated in an environment where a premium is placed on flashy one-shot workshops or conferences. Virtually every professional educational organization offers at least one conference a year. But if you ask the leaders of those organizations to show how those activities have impacted the practices of educators, they are unable to provide that data.

When most educators hear the term "professional development," they quickly envision a one-shot, "sit and get" workshop. Most educators will in fact tell you that professional development without ongoing coaching and support will not take root and change teacher practices, but requesting "training on" a particular strategy is the default for most educators. Since educators have usually been exposed to this type of one-shot training, they often do not know how to develop a structure in which teachers and leaders will actually improve their skills through systematic approaches like the activities described throughout this book.

There are some instances when it is beneficial for specific faculty members to attend one-shot training activities. There are some professionals in schools whose position calls for an extremely specialized skill set that is not shared by anyone else in the building. Examples of these professionals may include physical therapists, occupational therapists, teachers of students who are deaf/hard of hearing and communicate through sign language, and educational interpreters.

These individuals should certainly participate in the teacher groups and training activities that have been described in this book. They also need job specific training that they may not be able to get at their own school because they may be the only person in the school with their particular role. They need training and support in those highly specialized skills in order to impact their practices and the achievement of their students. The tendency will be for them to participate in one-shot training activities or conferences put on by their respective professional organizations.

This approach has no more likelihood of improving their specialized practices than it does for classroom teachers who are larger in number. They need to develop ongoing relationships with experts in their respective fields and with their colleagues who have similar jobs in other schools or school districts. As a leader in your school, help these professionals in establishing supportive networks for themselves so they can continually brainstorm with their colleagues. Much of this type of brainstorming can be accomplished online with additional opportunities for the professionals to meet face to face, perhaps in professional consortia.

When approached about attending a one-shot workshop that seems to provide specific information for these specialized professionals, ask them how they will access ongoing support, coaching, or brainstorming with like-minded colleagues as they implement the activities that are recommended at the conference.

MAKE ANNUAL PLANNING MEANINGFUL

Many schools have three-ring binders filled with exhaustive School Improvement Plans. In many instances, these plans were developed by select individuals who worked in isolation and then combined their efforts for the submission to the school district's central office or the state department of education. Once they are developed, most of these plans sit on the shelf in administrators' offices and are only pulled down when they have to be updated.

Countless hours that go into developing School Improvement Plans are wasted because the final document does not truly drive reform in the school. In many cases, the School Improvement Plans are full of layers of data analysis with long descriptions of the activities and programs that are implemented in the school.

Many School Improvement Plans essentially include an expansive laundry list of the programs and initiatives within the school. Priorities are not evident. No program or activity seems more important than any other. With that type of planning, all activities in a school will be implemented in the same way they were the previous year—with the same results. An efficient planning process should clearly designate a few priority areas for improvement based on student achievement. The areas of weakness should be precisely defined, and a few specific and meaningful activities should be completed to address those weaknesses.

Any reader should be able to connect the specific weaknesses with the logical and specific actions that will be implemented to address those weaknesses. The plan should include a description of how job-embedded professional development systems will be implemented so that teachers become more effective at implementing the prioritized activities. Annual plans are a case where less is truly more.

What happens when the school planning process lacks clarity and focus? The interventions are often not tightly aligned with the priority needs in the school. Take the example of Cooper Middle School. Cooper is a theoretical middle school in a large, urban school district and has approximately nine hundred students in the sixth, seventh, and eighth grades. For the past several years, the school has failed to meet the state's accountability standards. It is now considered a "needs improvement" school.

The student body is evenly composed of White, Hispanic, and African American students and virtually all of them are categorized as economically disadvantaged. Approximately 10 percent of the students are identified as having a disability. The state department of education reports the academic performance of several groups at Cooper: (1) all students, (2) Hispanic students, (3) African American students, (4) White students, (5) students with disabilities, and (6) students from economically disadvantaged circumstances. Three years of data are provided below that indicate the percentage of students in each subgroup that met or exceeded expectations on statewide assessments in English/language arts and mathematics.

Table 14.1. Percentage of Students who Met/Exceeded Expectations in Mathematics

	All Students	Hispanic	White	African American	Students with Disabilities	Economically Disadvantaged
Year I	49.7%	49.7%	49.2%	50.0%	27.8%	49.2%
Year II	44.9%	44.7%	44.2%	44.4%	25.6%	45.4%
Year III	36.5%	36.2%	35.1%	35.2%	21.1%	37.0%

Table 14.2. Percentage of Students Who Met/Exceeded Expectations in English/ Language Arts

	All Students	Hispanic	White	African American	Students with Disabilities	Economically Disadvantaged
Year I	65.0%	64.9%	64.8%	65.2%	38.7%	63.7%
Year II	64.9%	64.8%	65.0%	65.1%	39.2%	64.1%
Year III	68.4%	68.1%	68.5%	70.0%	45.9%	67.9%

The state department of education also published the following data that reflects the percentage of students in each group that were absent for more than fifteen days in the respective school year.

Additional data is also available. At Cooper Middle, 23 percent of students with disabilities spend at least 80 percent of their school day in general education classes. This is a reduction when compared to the two previous years.

When the leaders of Cooper Middle School were developing the School Improvement Plan, several initiatives were put in place. They decided to implement a gender-specific approach in their school. One-third of the school was established as the girls' academic team while another third of the school was established as the boys' academic team. The remaining students participated in co-ed classes. It was also determined that all teachers would loop with the students. The sixth-grade teachers would move to seventh grade when the students moved up at the end of the school year. They also implemented a double-dosing

Table 14.3. Percentage of Students Absent More Than Fifteen Days during the School Year

	All Students	Hispanic	White	African American	Students with Disabilities	Economically Disadvantaged
Year I	24.3%	23.9%	24.7%	23.6%	31.4%	25.3%
Year II	21.7%	21.3%	22.2%	21.0%	32.8%	22.0%
Year III	18.6%	18.5%	18.7%	17.0%	31.0%	18.5%

opportunity for students in mathematics. Students who did not meet expectations on the statewide assessment in mathematics participated in an additional math class instead of participating in an elective course.

There are significant problems with Cooper Middle School's School Improvement Plan. The data are stunningly clear. In fact, it is very rare that quantitative data tell a story with such clarity. Cooper Middle School has major difficulties with achievement in mathematics. Since Year I, the percentage of students who have met or exceeded expectations on statewide assessments has dropped drastically. This pattern is evident across every subgroup.

This is in stark contrast to the performance of the students in reading/English/language arts. For the two previous years, the data indicated relatively stable performance with an upswing for all subgroups during Year III. In fact, twice as many students met or exceeded standards in English/language arts than met or exceeded expectations in mathematics.

The data indicate that the challenges in math are systemic, not subgroup specific. Even though the performance of the students with disabilities is less than desirable, the math issue is not an issue only for students with disabilities. It is not a disability issue, but is a math issue.

There are additional data pieces that may explain some of the underperformance at Cooper Middle School. Even though the absentee rate has improved over the past few years, a large percentage of students in all subgroups are excessively absent, especially students with disabilities. In addition, there is a very low percentage of students with disabilities who are being educated in general education classes when compared to the placement patterns for students with disabilities across the country.

When you consider the achievement data for Cooper Middle School, it is apparent that there is one area that clearly needs attention above all others—mathematics. However, the School Improvement Plan does not reflect this focus. The leadership team has decided to implement gender-based school teams. There may not be anything wrong with gender-based education. In this case, it will only be effective at improving student achievement if it significantly changes the instruction that is provided in mathematics.

At Cooper, an extremely high percentage of students across all subgroups do not meet expectations in mathematics. This typically indicates that teachers do not have sufficient knowledge in the content area, in this scenario mathematics. Teachers do not have a deep and compelling understanding of the material that should be taught. They do not have expertise in the subject area and therefore are limited in delivering instruction that enables students to become sophisticated problem solvers.

With this lack of confidence in mathematics, teachers are providing surface-level information with ineffective teaching practices. They are not providing instruction that is guided by a deep and thorough understanding of the curricular standards (the "G" in GREAT instruction). They are also not providing instruction using research-based instructional strategies that require students to participate in rigorous activities (the "R" in GREAT instruction).

It would not be a surprise to observe mathematics classes across the school and to find two strategies monopolizing classroom activities—teacher lecture and student independent work. If this is in fact the case, then students would certainly not be engaged or excited by their class work in mathematics (the "E" in GREAT instruction). One might also assume that neither the teachers nor the leadership team are using formative assessment data to guide instruction. They are not using ongoing assessment data to implement instruction in flexible groups tailored to meet the specific needs of their students (the "A" and "T" in GREAT instruction). Had they been doing so, the targeted instruction would have resulted in higher levels of achievement across the board.

The leaders at Cooper are attempting to improve mathematics performance by providing a second dose of instruction in mathematics. As mentioned in the previous chapter, the double dosing in mathematics should be much more targeted than students' first segment in math. School leaders should work to ensure that students are provided GREAT instruction in their first math segment and that their second dose of math focuses on students' specific holes in their learning as determined by analyses of students' strengths and weaknesses.

In addition to focusing on mathematics instruction, Cooper Middle School should implement activities to address two additional needs. They should continue to implement activities that reduce the high absentee rates. The school has made progress in this area for several subgroups. They need to intensify their efforts to hopefully make a more drastic reduction in absentee rates.

The leadership team also must analyze why the interventions that are showing some progress for other subgroups are not having a positive impact on the disability subgroup. They need to analyze why there is a lack of progress for these students. Perhaps there are students who have ongoing health issues that are interfering with their ability to attend school. In this case, the school leaders need to build support systems so that students can participate in instruction, perhaps through hospital or home instruction when they must be absent.

Perhaps there is a pattern of suspending students who exhibit inappropriate behavior. This cycle of ineffective interventions may be inflating absentee rates. By analyzing the core issues, the leadership team will be able to design and implement interventions that will encourage students to attend school regularly, thereby giving them access to GREAT instruction.

There is another weakness in Cooper Middle School's School Improvement Plan. They have plans to loop the teachers with each consecutive year.

This approach is counterproductive when considering what it will take to steadily improve the practices of the teachers throughout the school. As mentioned in earlier chapters, teachers need the opportunity to learn about new practices, try out those practices, and analyze how those practices impact student performance. They need continuous opportunities to learn about the curriculum and to become more competent in that curriculum. They need the opportunity to brainstorm instruction with their peers and to learn formally and informally from those around them.

By utilizing a looping approach, the teachers will not be able to attain mastery of their content and pedagogy. Once they are gaining some traction and have made some real progress in their skillfulness and the ability to have a positive impact on student learning, they will have to start the process all over again as they learn new material for a different grade level. The looping approach will undermine the efforts to steadily and effectively improve the instructional practices of the teachers. Ultimately, Cooper Middle School is a clear example of a disconnection between the interventions and the school's needs. If the school implements its current plan, it will not make noticeable progress in student achievement.

There is another reason for developing School Improvement Plans that are concise and clear. All school stakeholders, including teachers, administrators, support personnel, central office staff, parents, school board members, and members of the community, should be able to pick up the School Improvement Plan and clearly understand how the school has been performing and the priorities for the school over the next few years.

For all school personnel, the School Improvement Plan should represent their charge. It should be posted in every classroom and should drive the small- and large-group teacher meetings that were discussed earlier. It should clearly document the instructional strategies that will be undertaken during the year and the job-embedded professional development activities to be implemented in order to improve the practices of school personnel.

The Improvement Plan should function as a public relations document. It should explain the major goals for the school and in a digestible format explain how the school is planning on meeting those goals. An effective Action Plan is provided for Cooper Middle School.

The Action Plan provides a clear and succinct road map that can be easily understood by all staff members and stakeholders. Instead of utilizing an Action Plan that describes all of the activities that will be conducted, Cooper Middle School clearly prioritizes those activities that will help them meet their school goals.

The Action Plan also reflects lots of work by the school staff. There are supporting documents that include a careful data analysis of student achievement

Textbox 14.1.   Cooper Middle School's Annual Plan of Action

Goals

Implement GREAT instruction routinely in every class. GREAT instruction is:
- Guided by the curriculum.
- Rigorous with research-based strategies.
- Engaging and exciting.
- Assessed continuously to guide instruction.
- Tailored through flexible groups.

Increase achievement in mathematics and English/language arts (ELA)
- At least 75 percent of the students in each subgroup of students will meet or exceed standards.

Reduce absentee rates
- No more than 12 percent of students in each subgroup will be absent more than fifteen days during the school year.

Increase the percentage of students with disabilities who are educated in general education classes
- At least 55 percent of the students with disabilities will spend five of their six instructional segments in general education classes.

Recent Status

Over the past few years, the mathematics achievement of students in all subgroups has decreased consistently. In English/language arts, students' academic performance has remained relatively stable with an upswing last year. Approximately twice as many students demonstrate proficiency in English/language arts than in math.

Although there has been improvement for almost all subgroups, the student absentee rate continues to be excessive.

The percentage of students with disabilities who are educated in general education classes is below state and national trends.

Next Steps

- Mathematics teachers will consistently provide instruction, guided by the performance standards, that requires the students to conduct sophisticated learning activities.

(continued)

Textbox 14.1. *(Continued)*

- The Mathematics Coordinator for the school district will provide one hour of training every other week for all math teachers that will include practice in mathematics content combined with investigations into research-based instructional strategies.
- The Principal, Mathematics Department Chair, Assistant Principal, and Instructional Coach will conduct two coaching observations a month with each mathematics teacher to assist them in incorporating their new skills.
- The results of common formative assessments will be reviewed every three weeks by teacher teams with a representative from the school's leadership team.
- Under the guidance of the Department Chair for English/language arts, the ELA teachers will meet every other week to analyze the performance of their students and to discuss research-based instructional activities, guided by the curriculum, which will improve student performance.
- A positive, schoolwide initiative will be implemented that will provide rewards for each student who has not been absent during the month. Layers of interventions (mentoring, partnerships with parents, and more frequent rewards) will be triggered for students who miss more than five days of school prior to December.
- There will be four training activities for all teachers on differentiating instruction for students with disabilities and co-teaching. Ongoing coaching and support will be provided by the Assistant Principal and Department Chair for Special Education.

---

and qualitative analysis of the school practices that are causing the student achievement levels, both good and bad. But the School Improvement Plan should be a document that propels action. Neither the school faculty nor members of the community are willing to wade through an expansive document to uncover the school's major goals or initiatives. This School Improvement Plan provides all stakeholders with the charge for the school for the next year.

A few comments should be made about the representation of students with disabilities in the school's Action Plan. This document is going to be shared across a broad audience of school personnel and members of the community. Therefore, a certain amount of sensitivity should be exercised.

First of all, students with disabilities should be fully included in the school's Action Plan. There should not be a separate Action Plan for students with disabilities. This will reinforce the idea that students with disabilities are students first before they are considered having disabilities. They are students like all other students. Their disabilities do not define them. They are part of the entire student body and should be treated as such.

The wording of the Action Plan should also be reviewed to ensure that students with disabilities are not cast in a negative light. In some schools, the disability subgroup is the only subgroup that did not meet accountability standards, therefore interfering with the school's ability to make the accountability benchmarks. In a school with that scenario, it would be easy for the Action Plan to read as if the students with disabilities are to blame for the school's underperformance.

The Action Plan documents the changes that are going to be made by the adults in the school. It should be reviewed to ensure that the members of the faculty or the community members could not read the document and cast blame on the students with disabilities.

According to federal law, there are also confidentiality considerations. Every child with a disability has rights to confidentiality. The fact that the student has a disability should not be shared with any person who is not directly involved with educating that child or supervising the education of that child. If a member of the leadership team is assigned to provide coaching consistently in a classroom, it is reasonable that the individual can be informed of the students with disabilities in the class. Therefore, the members of the leadership team who are connected to that classroom can be informed of a child's disability.

The Action Plan cannot include any personally identifiable information. It cannot share the names of any students with disabilities or provide enough information so that anyone could "figure out" who has a disability. The members of the leadership team should ensure that confidentiality is not compromised for students with disabilities through the Action Plan.

FOCUS ON INSTRUCTION, NOT PROCESS

As mentioned previously, schools are filled with initiatives that are seemingly in competition with each other. This perceived incongruence is a barrier to systematically improving student achievement. Many of these initiatives are funded with different pots of money, such as the various Title programs, and therefore have different funding sources and different documentation requirements. The Title I program requirements, for example, are quite different from the special education program requirements.

This lack of alignment is complicated all the more due to the fact that the various programs are usually administered by different departments within a school district. Many of the district offices layer additional documentation requirements on top of the federal requirements, very often for very good reasons. The problem with all of these requirements is that it is extremely

easy for school personnel to become focused on the process of administering the program rather than on the instruction that occurs on a daily basis in
classrooms.

Special education is a prime example of this problem. Prior to the mid-
1970s, school districts across the country were not obligated to provide
services to students with disabilities. In 1975, the federal law entitled the
Education for All Handicapped Children Act required that all school districts
across the country educate all students with disabilities. With that law, which
is extremely just, came layers of paperwork: student's evaluation processes,
individual planning activities for each student (Individual Education Program), and due process rights that ensure that students with disabilities are
afforded a "free and appropriate public education."

Through the years, the federal legislation has been reauthorized, most recently
in 2004, and is now referred to as the Individuals with Disabilities Education
Improvement Act. In addition to the mandated processes that are established for
every individual child, which become more complex with every reauthorization
of the law, there are also requirements at the district level.

School districts must collect large data sets for reports such as the percentage of students with disabilities who are suspended or expelled for disciplin-
ary reasons, the percentage of students with disabilities who are educated in
general education classes for certain percentages of the day, and the ethnic
distribution of various disabilities.

The data for students with disabilities can inform a school district that it is
educating a higher percentage of students with disabilities in segregated, pull-out
special education classes than other districts in their state and across the country.
This is very meaningful information that can guide the school district in determining that equipping teachers to provide effective instructional programs for
students with disabilities in general education classes is a priority.

Although the documentation and the required processes have a specific
rationale and purpose, the sheer magnitude of the requirements can easily
overshadow the instructional programs. Administrators, teachers, and parents
can easily become bogged down in the administrative processes and lose focus on the real purpose of equitable education—to improve the achievement
and opportunities for students with disabilities.

What should a school district or individual school do to remedy this problem? First of all, it is critical that specific members of the school district
have a clear understanding of the origin and specific requirements of each
program. Depending on the program in question, some of the requirements
will be defined by the United States Department of Education with additional
requirement perhaps added by the state department of education and the local
school district. Some have been in effect for many years.

At the district level, personnel should have a deep understanding of the federal requirements. This should be the starting point. They should also consider how these requirements can be reported. Is the process at the district level for the schools more cumbersome than it has to be to meet requirements? Many times, especially as personnel changes occur at the school and district level, documentation and processes are maintained long after the original requirement has been removed. By having a deep understanding of the actual requirements from the funding source, school and district personnel can continually work to make the actual processes implemented in schools as streamlined as possible.

Ultimately, the implementation of processes should aim to meet the requirements as easily as possible while providing meaningful information. By minimizing the documentation and simplifying the processes, the district and school personnel can focus their time and effort on the instructional programs. Effort should also be placed into aligning all of the various documentation requirements.

FOCUS ON IMPROVING INSTRUCTION EVEN WHEN IMPLEMENTING STRUCTURAL CHANGES

Over the past decade many middle and high schools have transitioned from a schedule in which the students spent approximately one hour in each subject area to a block schedule in which students have extended time, perhaps ninety minutes to two hours, in each academic period, with fewer classes each day. The rationale for the block schedule is that there is time to delve deeper in the subject matter and complete more complex and rigorous activities. With the lengthened periods, teachers have the opportunity to provide hands-on activities in which students use critical thinking skills to apply the academic content.

In the schools where block scheduling changed instruction in that way, student achievement increased. In many schools, perhaps most schools that adopted block scheduling, classroom instruction did not change. Teachers provided the same instruction, just for longer periods. Therefore, there was no significant increase in student achievement. Even though there are some other benefits to block scheduling, such as a reduction in the amount of time that students spend in hallways, it is reasonable to ask whether the shift in the schedules and all of the person-hours that went into that effort were a good investment.

Initially, school leaders had to spend an extraordinary amount of time learning to organize their building in a block schedule. That activity, which seems natural at this point for many schools, involved a steep learning curve. School leaders had to reorganize how teachers and students were positioned on the schoolwide schedule and how that schedule impacted all activities throughout the school. Teachers also participated in staff development activities regarding block scheduling. Entire faculties participated in workshops that described how this approach benefits students and faculties.

If there was not a corresponding change in student achievement (because instruction was not fundamentally changed), is it unreasonable to say that all of those person-hours were wasted? There is nothing inherently wrong with either block scheduling or traditional scheduling, but this does illustrate the point that school improvement efforts that do not ultimately focus on improving classroom instruction will not have a noticeable impact on student achievement.

When implementing structural changes, whether converting to block schedules, remapping the organization chart, or changing the graduation requirements, for example, maintain a diligent focus on improving classroom instruction. The school leadership team should not limit its evaluation of the structural changes to how well those changes are being implemented.

In the case of block scheduling, for example, do not merely evaluate whether teachers and students are adapting to their new schedule. Make sure that you evaluate the corresponding changes in classroom instruction and student achievement. Conduct classroom observations to ensure that teachers are implementing the various components of GREAT instruction with greater fidelity than they did when there was a traditional schedule. Analyze formative and summative data to determine if students are exhibiting higher levels of achievement. Structural changes will not ultimately improve student achievement if there is not a consistent improvement in classroom instruction.

If you are currently implementing a block schedule in your school, it is not necessarily a good idea to convert back to a traditional schedule. That will not necessarily change instruction either. If student achievement is relatively flat, then you must build the systems described in this book to change the instructional practices across the school.

FOCUS ON CHANGING PRACTICES, NOT "CULTURE"

Many books have been written about our need to improve the culture of our schools. Administrators in schools that have traditionally shown systemic weaknesses discuss how they must change the culture of their school before they will see significant improvements in student achievement. This line of thinking dictates that culture must change before changes in instruction and student learning can be expected. The problem with this reasoning is that it is based on the premise that educators must somehow change the way they think before leaders can expect changes in their practices.

Another problem with this line of thinking is that a school's culture is very difficult to define. Some administrators will say that the culture of their school has improved when there is not a corresponding improvement in student achievement.

The truth is that a culture changes after adult practices are improved. A school's culture changes when teachers change from implementing weak instruction to implementing GREAT instruction and when the school's leaders spend their time building and implementing layers of support for that instruction. An improved culture is a side effect of drastically improving what happens in classrooms. By implementing systematic steps to improve instruction across the school, you ultimately impact culture.

Questions for Reflection

1. Consider the professional development activities that have been undertaken by your faculty. Have the professional development activities primarily focused on internal and external one-shot workshops? If so, were those activities effective at improving educators' practices and student performance? If not, describe why those professional development activities were ineffective.
2. Is your annual planning process effective? Have you seen significant progress over the past few years or does the planning process seem ineffective at establishing a blueprint that will lead to observable improvements in instruction and thereby student performance? Explain your answer.
3. Is your School Improvement Plan a concise document that clearly describes the priorities for instructional improvement? Is that document used and understood by all stakeholders, including administrators, teachers, students' families, and members of the community, to drive their actions?
4. In your school, is there an imbalanced focus on processes rather than instruction? Does the completion of those processes seem to have a positive or negative impact on student achievement? Describe how some processes can be eliminated or streamlined so that the school faculty can have an increased and diligent focus on instruction.
5. Are the special education leaders in your school and district providing support to two main areas—implementing and monitoring paperwork

processes while being a valuable member of the school leadership that builds and implements school improvement efforts?

6. Describe some of the structural changes that have been implemented in your school during the past few years. Were those changes accompanied by corresponding improvements in classroom instruction? If not, describe why that is. Also describe how current structural changes can be used to further the cause of implementing GREAT instruction.

7. In your school, are you focusing on changing culture rather than changing adult practices? If so, describe how you can focus on changing adult practices (both teachers and leaders) toward GREAT instruction.

Chapter Fifteen

Unrelenting Persistence

Throughout this book, it is clear that a school must diligently focus on providing GREAT instruction in order to radically improve the achievement of all students, including students with disabilities. To be honest, it will take more than diligence. It will take persistence, unrelenting persistence. Countless initiatives, processes, and requirements will try to distract you. The daily demands of running a school will tempt you to lose your focus. Sometimes, well-meaning personnel with misaligned initiatives will try to take you off of your game.

You must show unrelenting persistence and not be deterred. You will not lose your focus. You will consistently lead your school toward GREAT instruction. As the leadership team, you must create a consistent and coherent vision of the components of effective instruction for your leaders and your teachers. Then you must methodically build and implement systems of support so that all personnel gradually improve their practices.

You must not be satisfied with providing one-shot workshops and hoping that teachers implement better practices. You must build systems of ongoing professional development that include brainstorming, coaching, and support. You must monitor formative data to ensure that students are mastering the curriculum. You must ensure that every student with a disability who should be educated in a general education class is given that opportunity. You must tirelessly focus on improving instruction in every classroom across your school. Your persistence must be wrapped up in a positive and contagious attitude. But you must show uncompromising persistence nonetheless.

According to L. Brown (personal communication, January 15, 2004), every school improvement initiative needs a "project warrior" who will continuously carry the torch for the new effort. These people will not allow their schools to lose focus. They will maintain the momentum. They will ask their colleagues about implementation. They will review ongoing data. They will analyze both teacher practices and student performance. They will not let the initiative fade away to be replaced by the next initiative. They will stay the course.

All members of the leadership team—the principal, assistant principals, instructional coaches, and lead teachers—must be "project warriors" who show positive, unrelenting persistence about improving instruction. You must be the cheerleaders for every step of the improvement activities. You must be the ones who continually remind all personnel about what can happen in your school. When teachers and leaders are discouraged, you must remind them of the stakes and paint the landscape of possibilities. You must encourage them so that they believe that it can be done and provide gentle but real pressure to be sure it gets done.

Even when faced with the setbacks that will inevitably come, you must continue to move the school forward with a diligent focus on improving instruction. You must be the coach, the cheerleader, and the monitor. You must make it clear that you will not be distracted. You will not be sidetracked. You will develop GREAT instruction in every classroom. You will focus your school and you will radically improve student achievement.

You must also be the visionary. There are many schools that have a long history of poor performance. Those schools are often filled with personnel who cannot even envision the possibilities for their school. In some high schools, for example, administrators and teachers cannot see what a great high school can be. They assume that more than half of the students are just going to be disengaged. They assume that all classrooms must be filled with the teacher lecturing from the front of the room while a large percentage of the students disregard the instruction. Those teachers expect that students will not be enthralled with their work, and they mark it as a successful day if there aren't any major disruptions in the class.

Your leadership must enlist the faculty in what is possible. High schools should be places where students walk into their classrooms and jump into rigorous and engaging activities. They should be working in large and small groups and discussing and solving complex problems in all subject areas. Students should be engaged in different sides of political arguments and get involved in different political causes. They should develop the math skills and build complex structures to test out those math skills. They should be engaged with great literature and compare the tone, message, and plot of historical literature with the work of contemporary authors.

A high school student, and students in all grades, should have school days filled with enlightening discussions, interesting investigations, and multifaceted demonstrations of what they have learned. Students should feel challenged and supported with novel and interesting activities as they pursue deep understandings of their content area. All schools can be exciting places where students enjoy their daily activities and grow academically and socially.

There are also many educators who do not believe that students with disabilities can achieve at high levels. They think that it is inevitable that students with disabilities will underperform. As the leader, you must inspire, convince, and require all teachers to provide engaging and effective instruction to all students, including their students with disabilities. Teachers must have high expectations for students with disabilities and enable those students to meet those expectations. We, as leaders, cannot allow teachers to accept low achievement because they think it is unavoidable.

Your leadership team must clearly communicate the possibilities for all schools: elementary, middle, and high schools. You must also communicate the possibilities for all students. You must give your faculty the permission to dream big, to envision what kind of school you can become and how you can reach all students. You must set a course and then be unrelenting in your persistence to create those practices in your school. You have to envision it, enlist others, and then make it happen. You have to provide great leadership so that you can have GREAT instruction in every class in your school.

References

About the national reading panel. (2001). Retrieved June 27, 2006, from www.nation-alreadingpanel.org/NRPAbout/about nrp.htm.

Baron, K. (2007). Personal communication with the author.

Brown, L. (2004). Personal communication with the author.

Bryar, M. (November 2006). *Once upon a time in Georgia.* Presented at the Georgia Council for Administrators of Special Education Statewide Conference.

Bryar, M., O'Connor, J., O'Connell, G., Brown, L., Mauney, H., & Swan, B. (2005). *Scaling up and evaluating professional development: How the Georgia SIG has impacted hundreds of schools through professional development initiatives.* Presented at the National State Improvement Grants Conference.

Burrello, L., Burrello, J., & Friend, M. (1996). *The power of two: Making a difference through co-teaching* (videotape). Bloomington: Indiana University.

California Department of Education. (2007). *State accountability report card (2006–2007).* Retrieved January 9, 2009, from www.cde.ca.gov/ta/ac/sc/documents/reportcard0607.pdf.

Cranium. (n.d.). Super Fort. Retrieved April 7, 2007, from store.cranium.com/catalog/product_info.php?ePath=1_136&products_id=881.

Education for All Handicapped Children Act—P.L. 94-142. (1975). 94th Congress of the United States.

Eggers, L. (1993). Personal communication with the author.

Fuchs, L., & Fuchs, D. (n.d.). *What is scientifically-based research on progress monitoring?* Retrieved May 6, 2007, from www.studentprogress.org/library/articles.asp#formative.

Georgia Department of Education. (2008a). *2007–2008 Special education annual report.* Retrieved January 10, 2009, from www.gadoe.org/ReportingFW.aspx?Page Req=105&PTID=CTID=41&Source=Regular%Diplomas&PID=38&CountyId=6 11&T=1&FY=2008.

Georgia Department of Education. (2008b). *2007–2008 Special education annual report.* Retrieved January 27, 2009, from www.gadoe.org.

Gloeckler, L. (2006). *Rigor, relevance, and relationships—Where do students with disabilities fit?* Presented at the Fourteenth Annual Model Schools Conference.

Hart, B., & Risley, R. T. (1995). *Meaningful differences in the everyday experience of young American children.* Baltimore: Paul H. Brookes.

Holland, L. (2005). Personal communication with the author.

Hughes, C. A., & Archer, A. (in press). *Teaching students with learning difficulties: Making instruction effective and explicit.* New York: Guilford Press.

Illinois State Board of Education (2008). *2006-2007 Annual state report on special education.* Retrieved January 5, 2009, from webprod1.isbe.net/LEAProfile/search Criteria1.aspx.

Individuals with Disabilities Education Act—P.L. 108-446. (2004). 108th Congress of the United States.

Marzano, R. J., Pickering, D. J., & Pollock, J. E. (2001). *Classroom instruction that works: Research-based strategies for increasing student achievement.* Alexandria, VA: Association for Supervision and Curriculum Development.

National Center on Student Progress Monitoring. (n.d.). *Resources: Curriculum-based measurement at the secondary-school level.* Retrieved May 6, 2007, from www .studentprogress.org/library/articles.asp#formative.

National Institute of Child Health and Human Development. (2000). *Report of the National Reading Panel. Teaching children to read: An evidence-based assessment of the scientific research literature on reading and its implications for reading instruction: Reports of the subgroups* (NIH Publication No. 00-4754). Washington, DC: U.S. Government Printing Office.

National Mathematics Advisory Panel. (2008). *Foundations for success: The final report of the national mathematics advisory panel.* Washington, DC: U.S. Department of Education.

No Child Left Behind Act—P.L. 107-110. (2001). 107th Congress of the United States.

O'Connor, J. L., & Williams, L. C. (2006). *Students with disabilities can make AYP: What every school leader should know.* Atlanta: Georgia Department of Education.

O'Connor, S. (1998). Personal communication with the author.

Ripley, A. (2008, December 8). Can she save our schools? *Time,* 36–44.

Showers, B., & Joyce, B. (1996). *The evolution of peer coaching* (electronic version). *Educational Leadership, 53*(6), 12–15.

U.S. Department of Education. (2004). *26th Annual report to Congress on the implementation of the Individuals with Disabilities Education Act,* vol. 1. Washington, DC: U.S. Department of Education.

U.S. Department of Education. (2005). *27th Annual report to Congress on the implementation of the Individuals with Disabilities Education Act.* Retrieved November 10, 2008, from www.ed.gov/about/reports/annual/osep/2005/parts-b-c/27th-vol-1.doc.

U.S. Department of Education (2006). *Highly qualified teachers for every child.* Retrieved May 4, 2007, from www.ed.gov/nclb/methods/teachers/stateplanfacts.

Villa, A., Thousand, J., & Nevin, A. (2004). *A guide to co-teaching: practical tips for student learning.* Thousand Oaks, CA: Corwin Press.

What Works Clearinghouse. (n.d.). *Who we are.* Retrieved June 22, 2008, from www .whatworks.ed.gov.

About the Author

John O'Connor has led school improvement initiatives at the state and local levels during his twenty years in public education. He is currently the Executive Director for Special Services with the DeKalb County School System in metro Atlanta. He has provided training to more than one hundred district, state, and national audiences. This is his third book. He cowrote *Students with Disabilities Can Make AYP* and wrote *Turning Average Instruction into GREAT Instruction*. O'Connor lives in Stockbridge, Georgia, with his wife, Shawn, and two sons, J. T. and Luke.